USE AS CALENDAR COVER-UPS

Choose one pattern for monthly cover-ups on calendar dates. Duplicate the pattern on regular white paper, construction paper or lightweight tagboard. If possible, laminate these calendar cover-up patterns so they can be used again.

USE AS NAME TAGS

Choose one pattern to use as name tags for special events. Follow the same steps used to make calendar cover-ups. Print the names on the completed tags.

USE AS BULLETIN BOARD THEMES

Choose a pattern to use as a bulletin board theme. Enlarge the pattern by use of an overhead projector and the following steps:

1. Using an overhead pen, trace the pattern on a clear sheet of acetate, a plastic bag or wax paper.
2. Tape a sheet of paper or tagboard on the wall.
3. Place the acetate sheet on the overhead projector and project the picture onto the paper or tagboard.
4. Move the overhead projector forward to make the picture smaller or move it back to enlarge the picture.
5. Trace around the projected image.

Once the enlarged image has been traced, use crayons, water pastels, colored chalk or markers to complete the sketch. Cut out the finished bulletin board picture and attach it to the desired bulletin board area. The finished picture can be used above a calendar or as part of a theme used to motivate students. Trace a related pattern for each student in the classroom, or allow students to trace their own. Label these patterns with the students' names. Inform the students of the goal they must reach (example: a perfect score on a spelling test). Once the students achieve this set goal, they may display their related patterns on the bulletin board.

USE AS STORY STARTERS

Choose a pattern for a story starter. Enlarge the pattern using the overhead projector. Print a related word list on the enlarged pattern. Students may use the story starter to create their own stories.

USE AS RACE GAMES

Choose one pattern to use as the start position of the game. Choose another pattern to use as the finish position of the game. Use the third pattern to make a path for the game. Arrange the pattern into a game format. (See example below.)

Directions: Put the marker at start position. Move the marker across the gameboard as turns are taken. First person to reach finish is the winner.

Variations for Race Gameboards:

1. Attach the gameboard to a bulletin board. Change the board for different holidays.
2. Design the game on tagboard for small groups or on file folders for partners.
3. Make a transparency of the gameboard and project it onto the chalkboard to play with the entire class or in small groups.
4. Paint the gameboard on the floor of your classroom with white shoe polish.

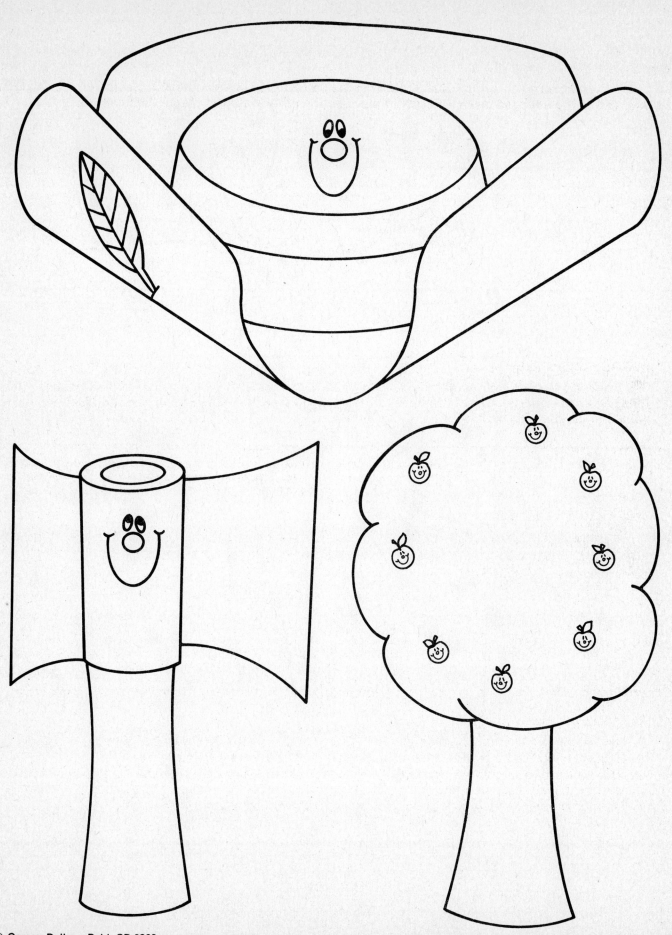

3

4

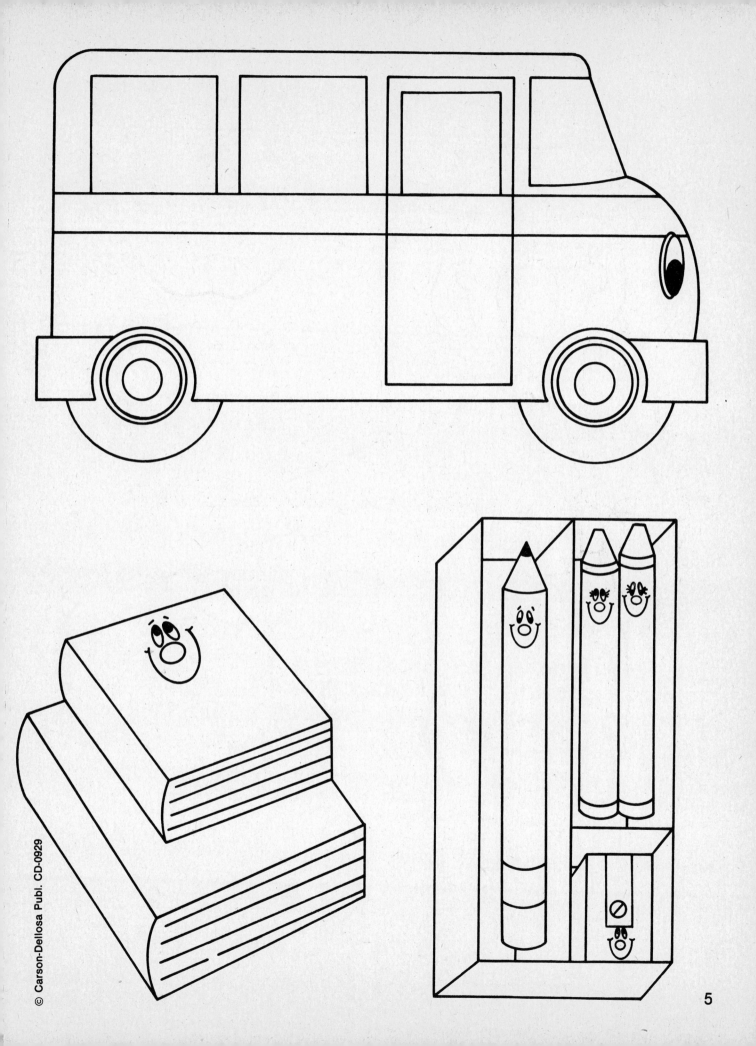

5

6

8

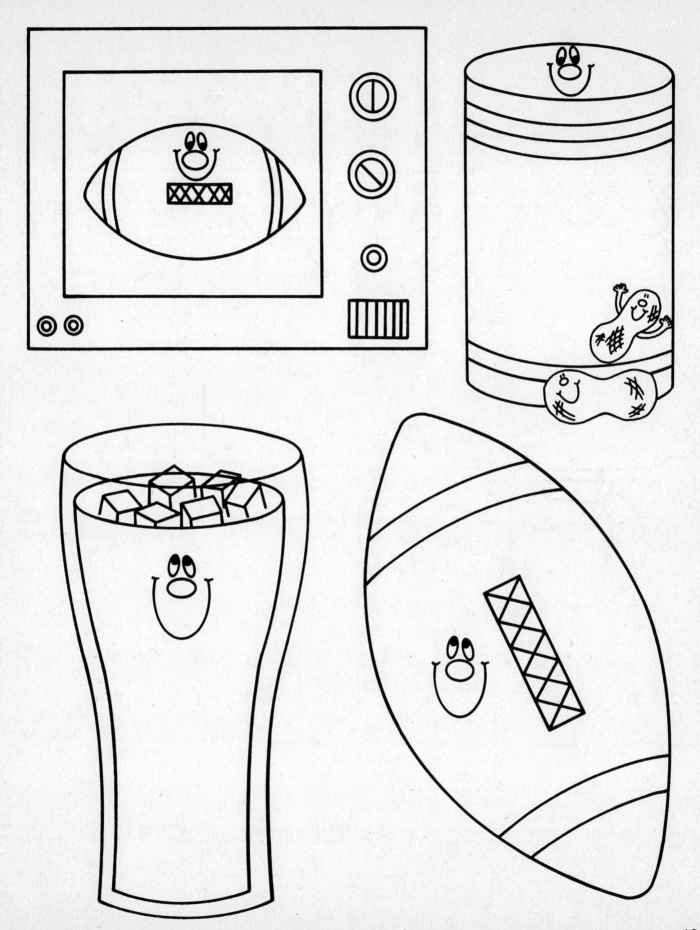

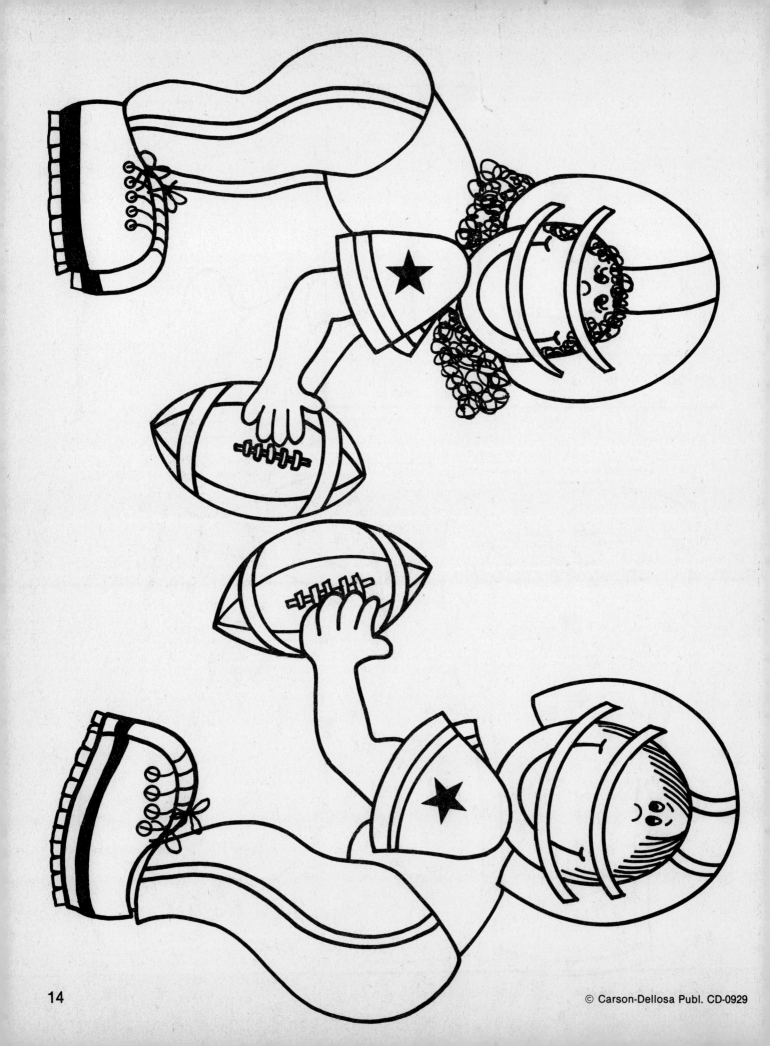

14

16

17

18

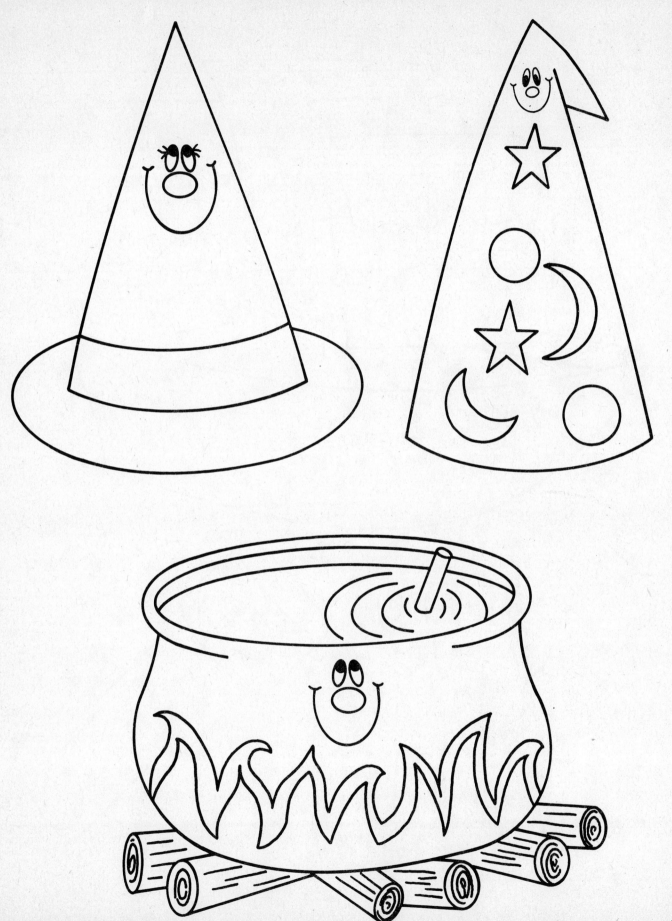

19

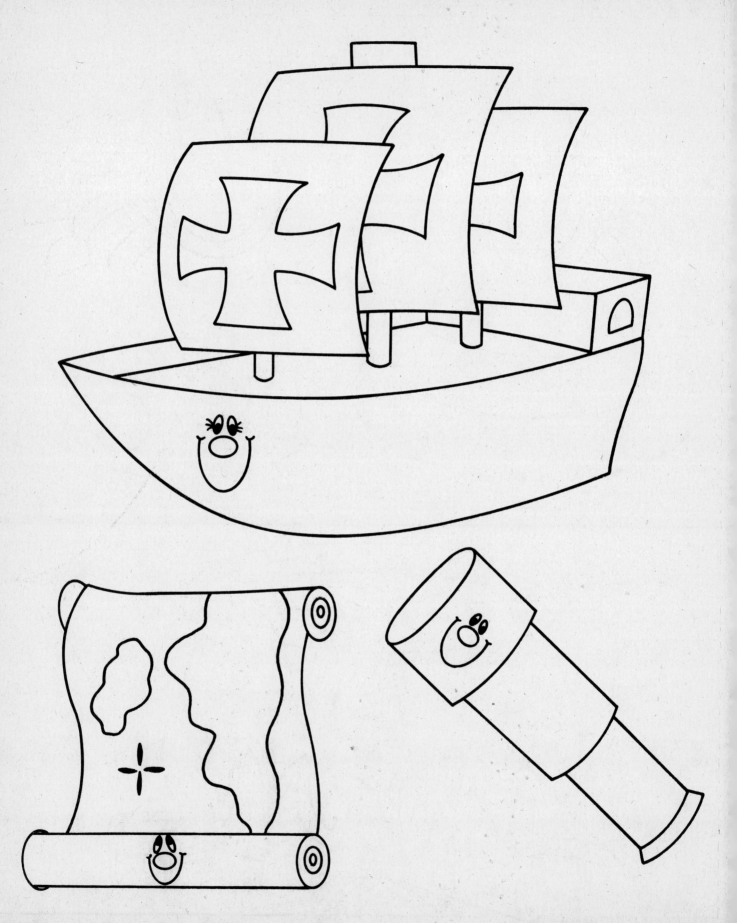

24

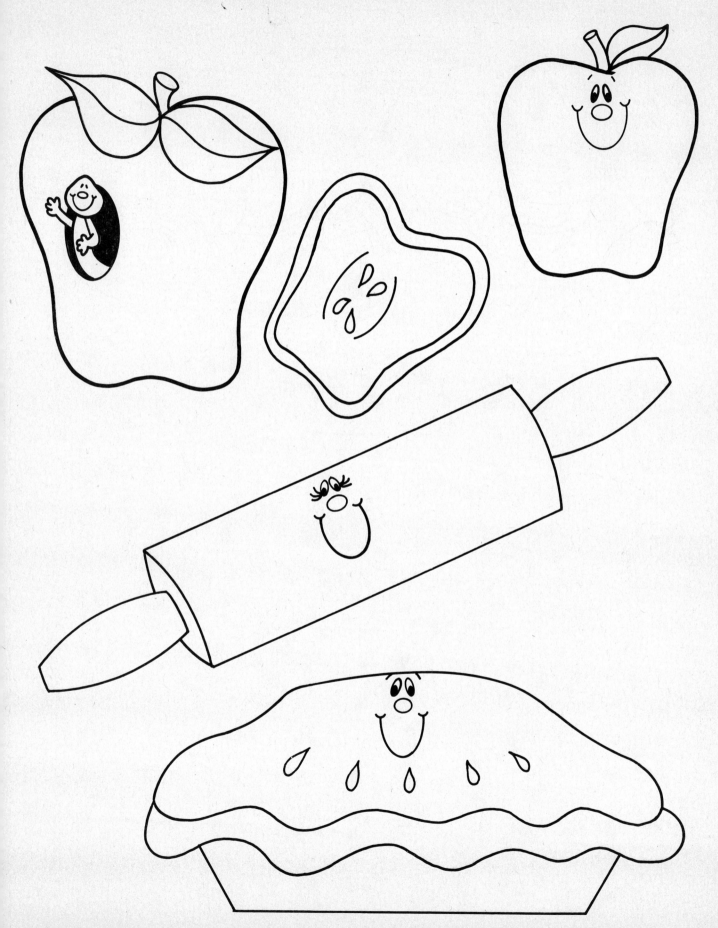

28

30

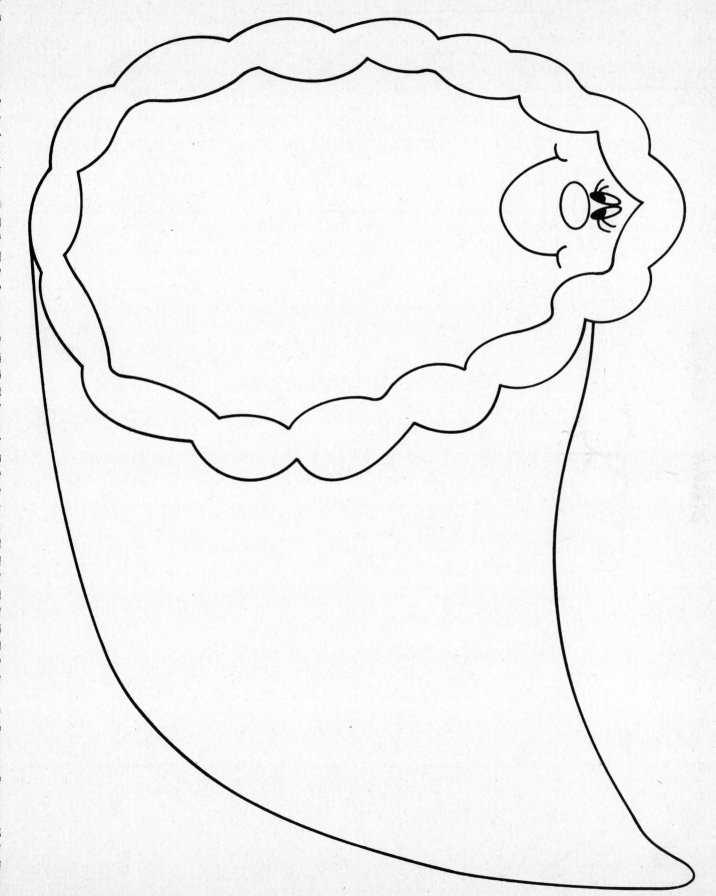

31

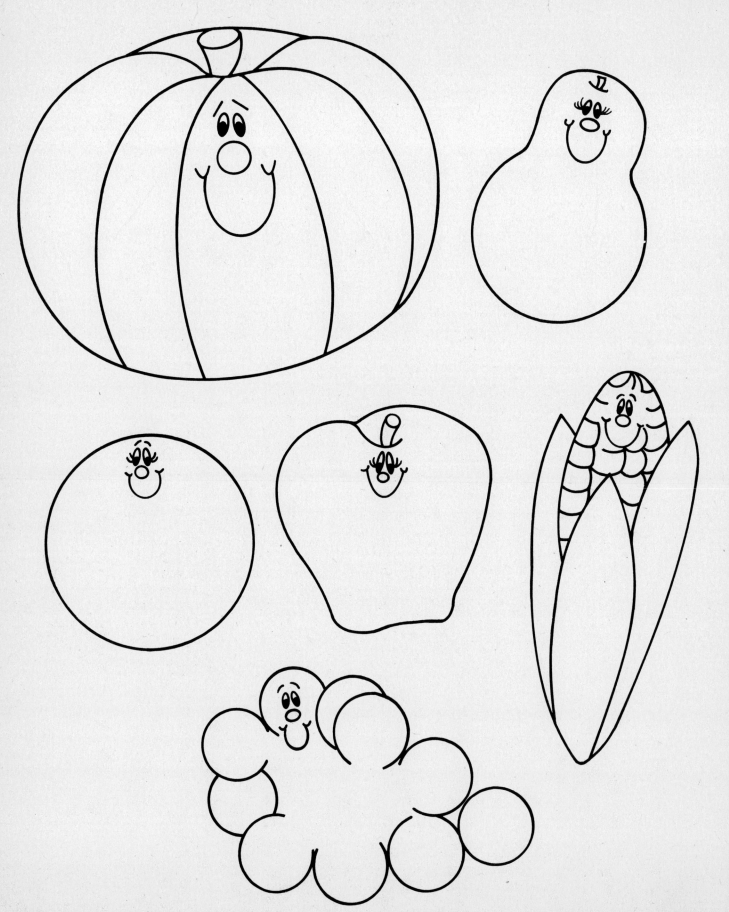

32

Happy Thanksgiving !!

35

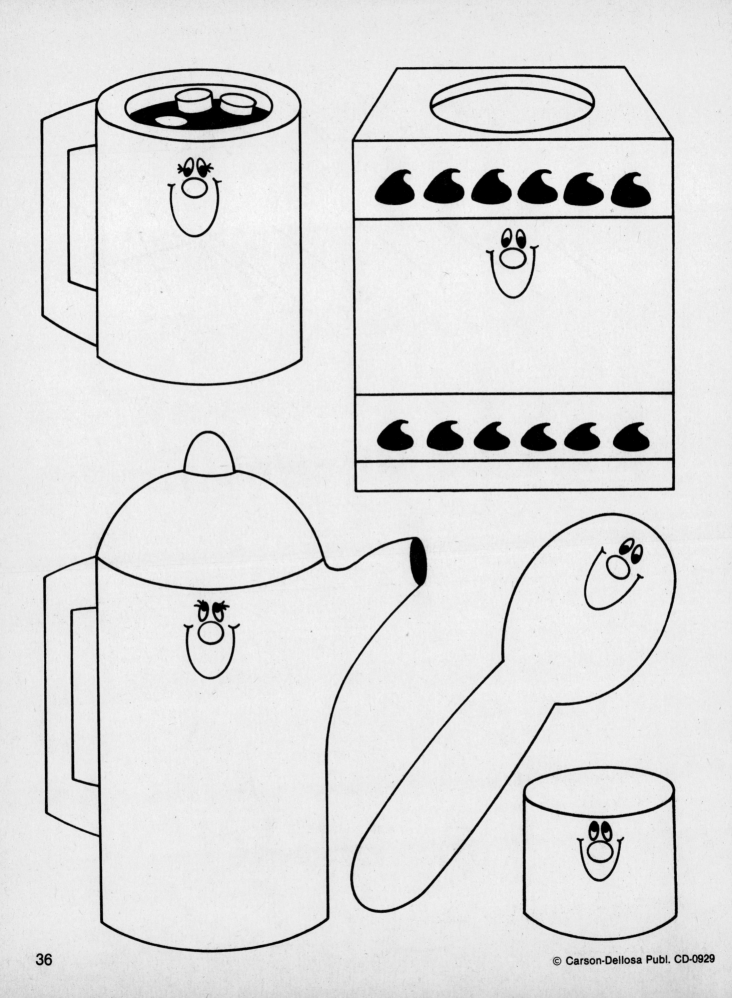

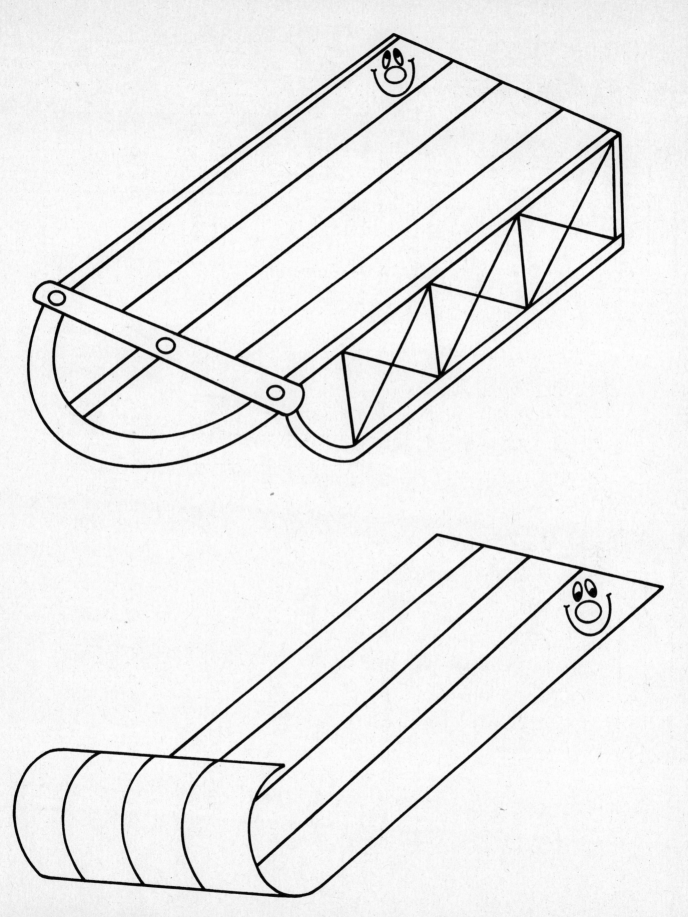

37

38

40

41

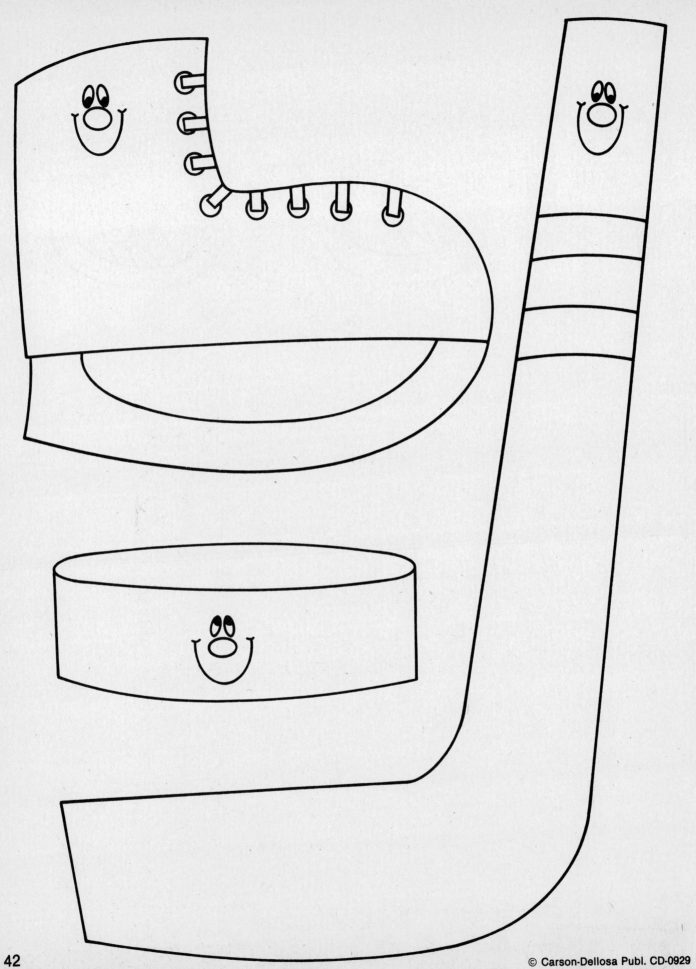

42

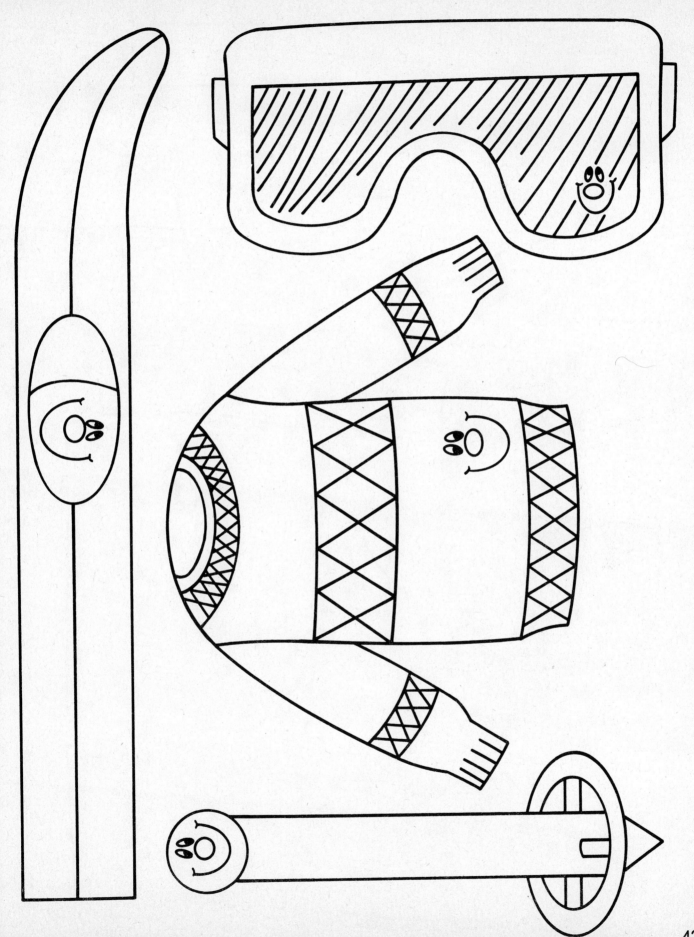

43

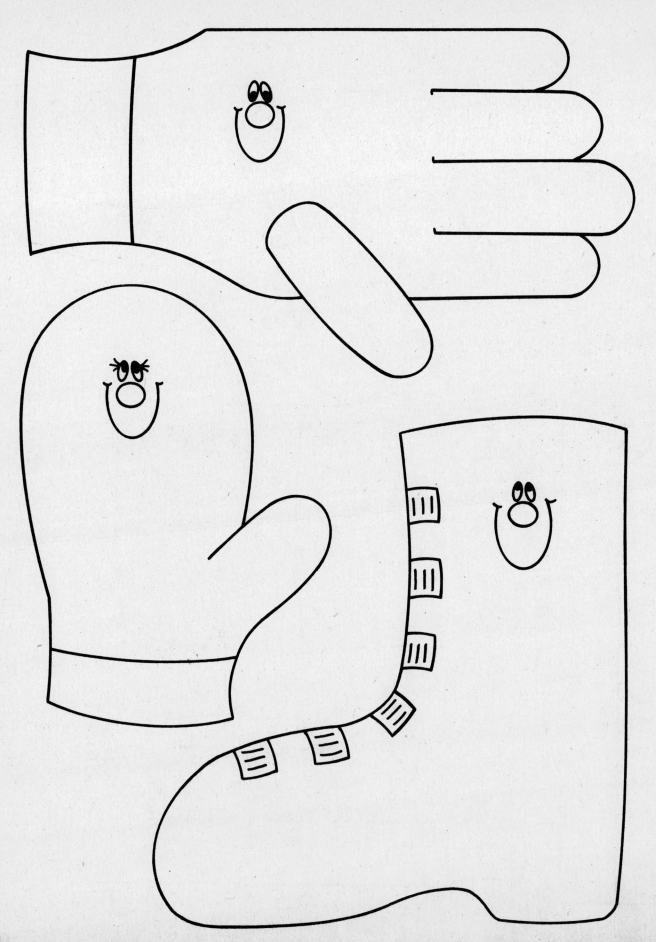

44

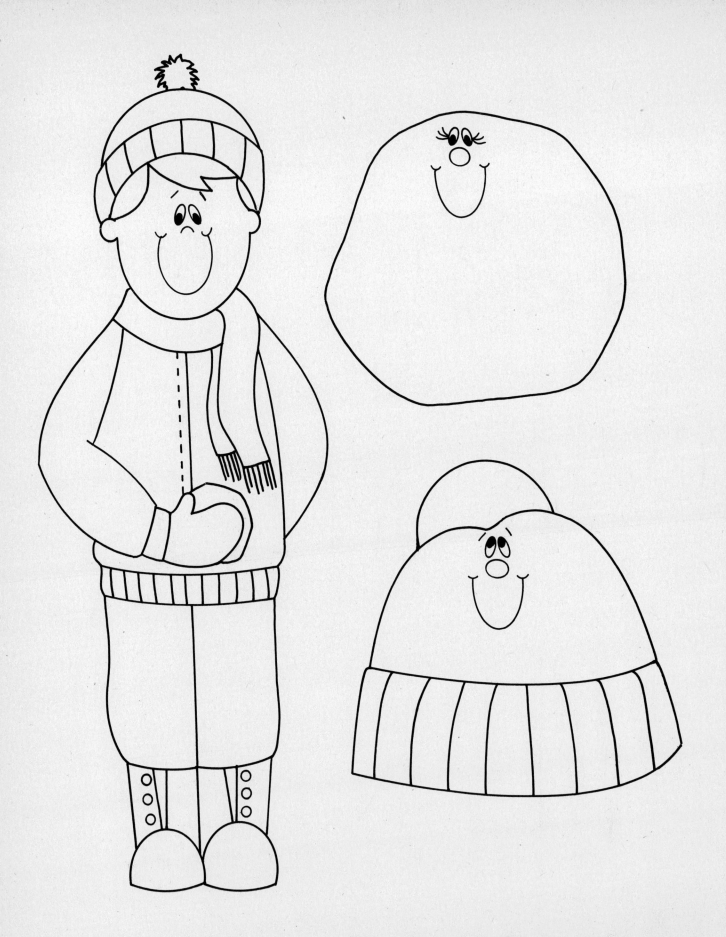

50

Wish List

51

Dear Santa,

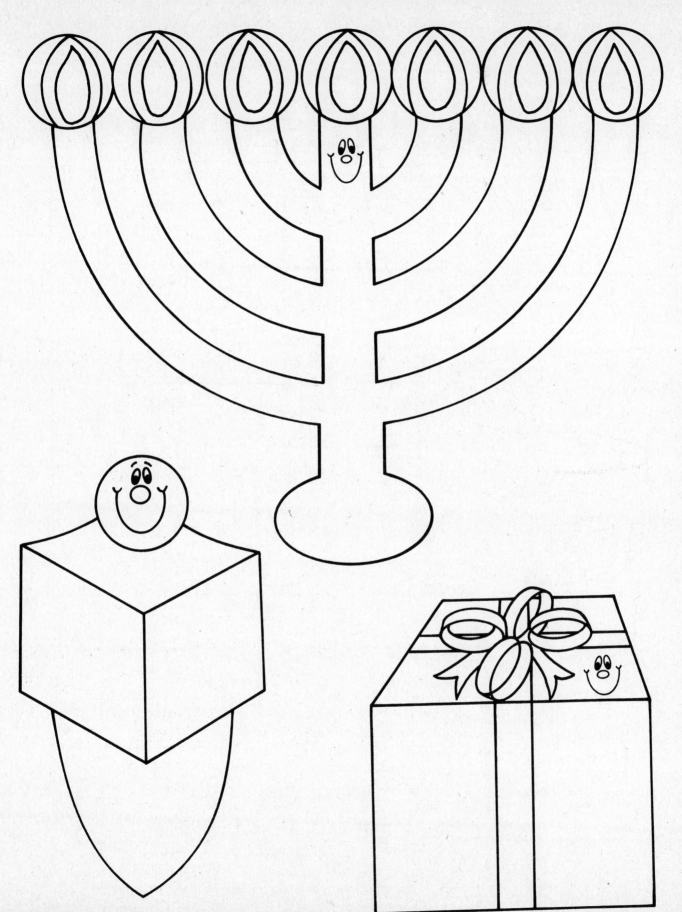

54

55

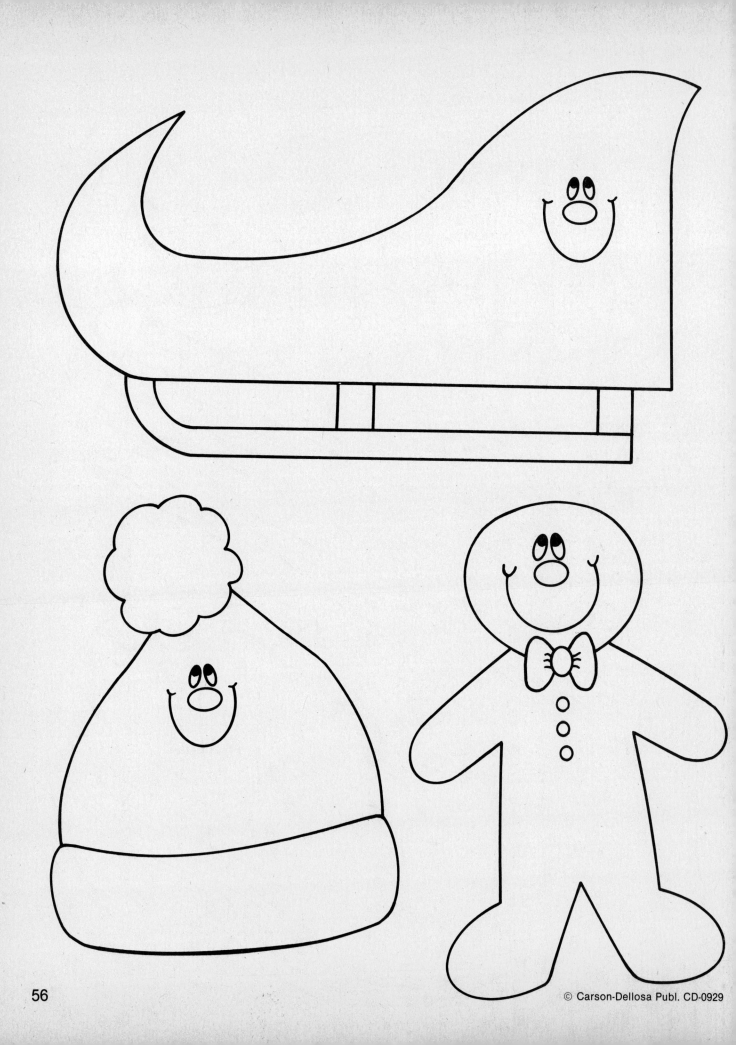

56

57

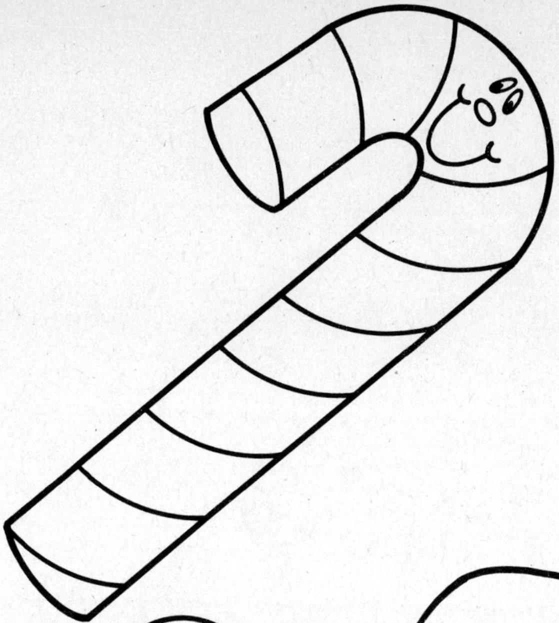

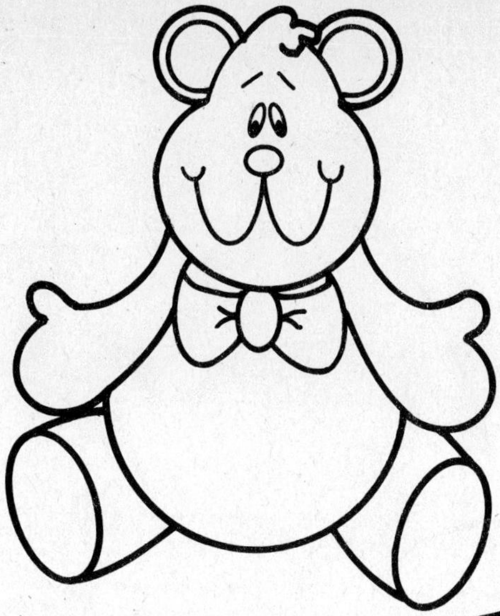

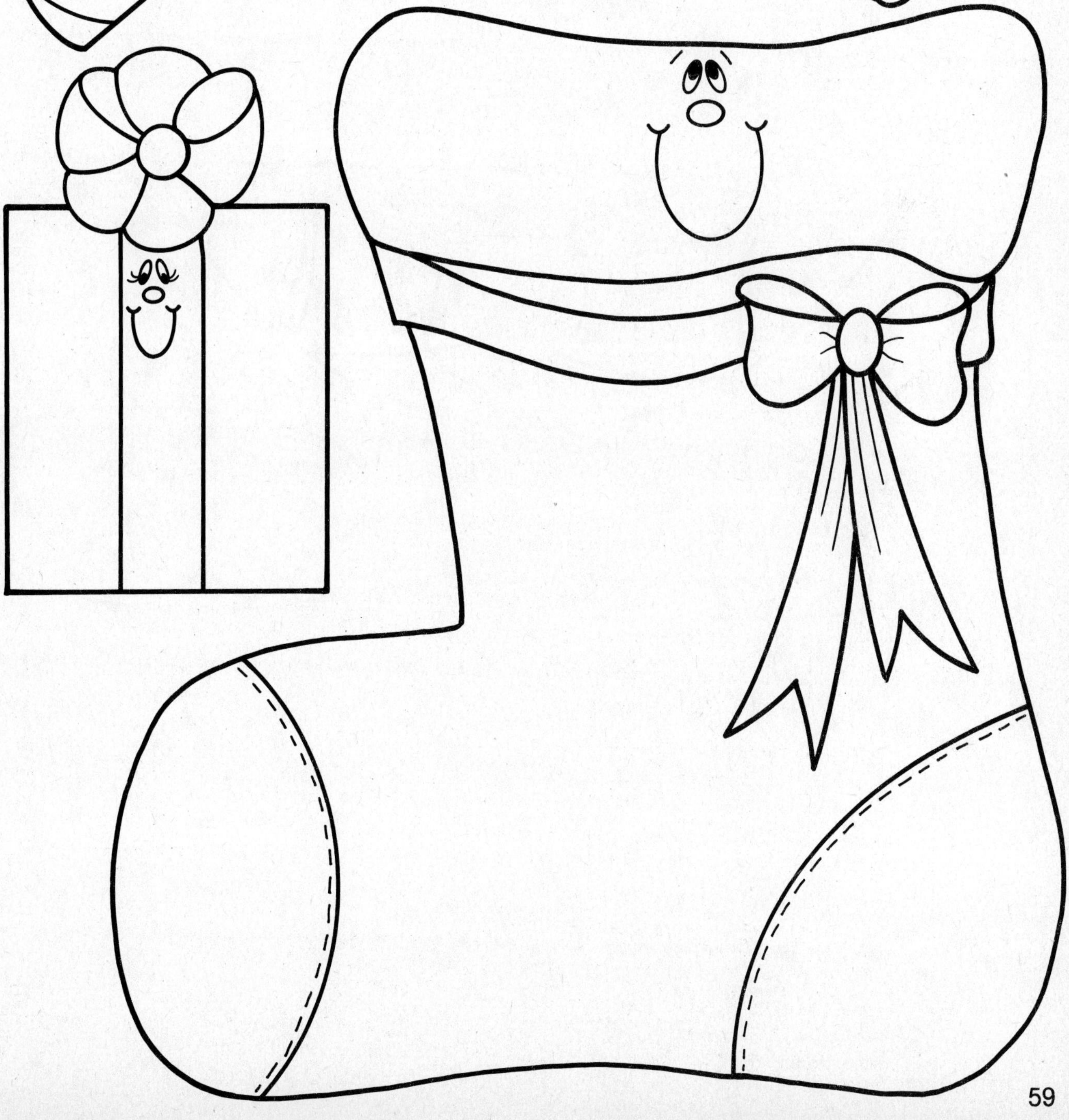

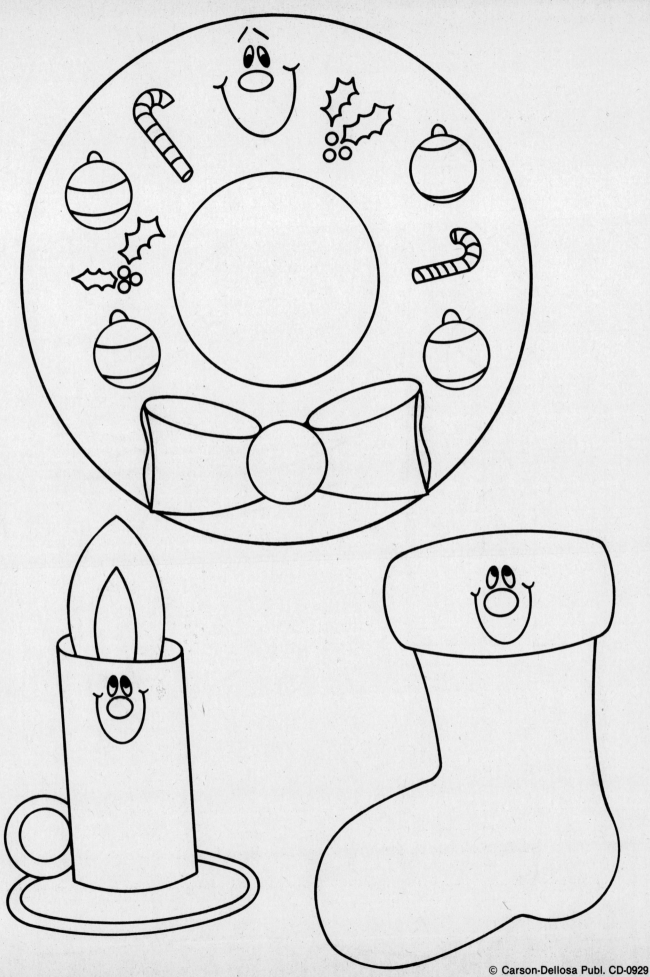

60

62

63

64

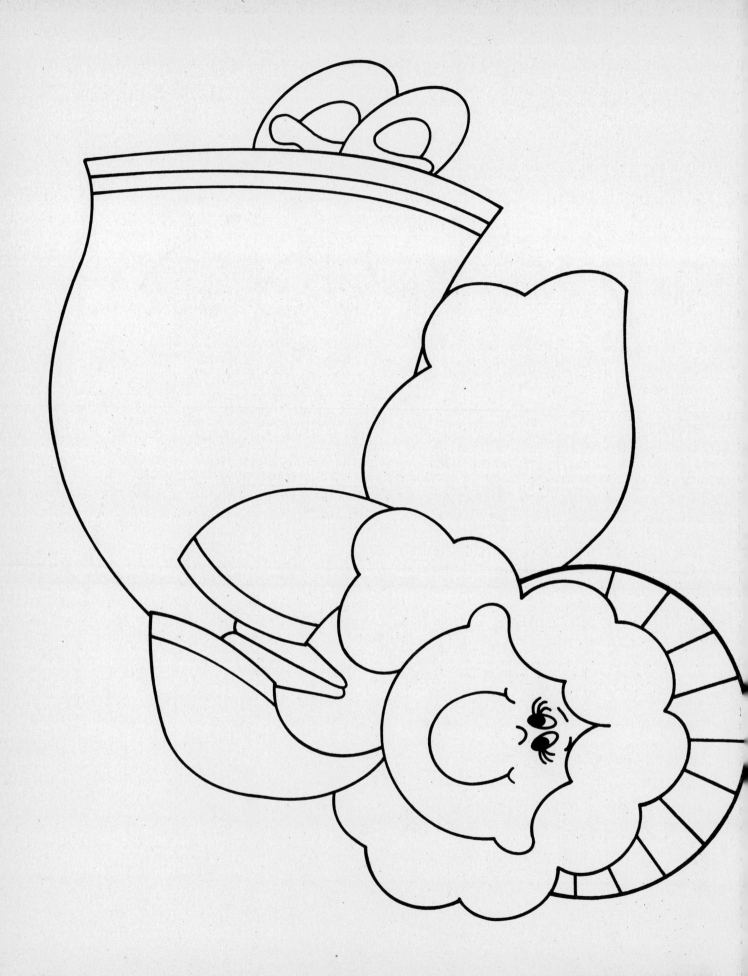

70

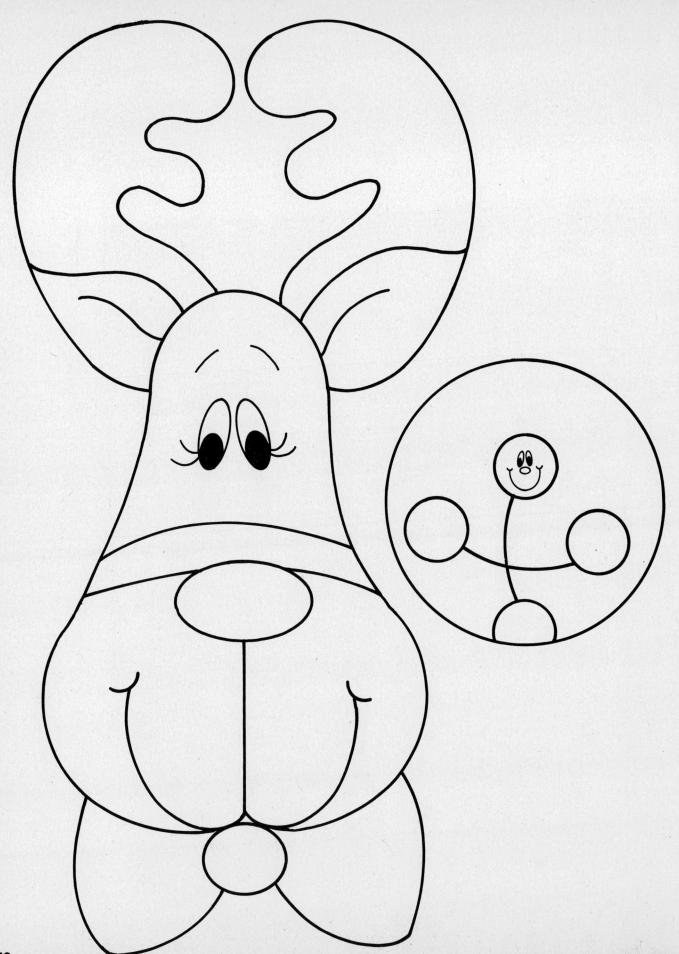

72

74

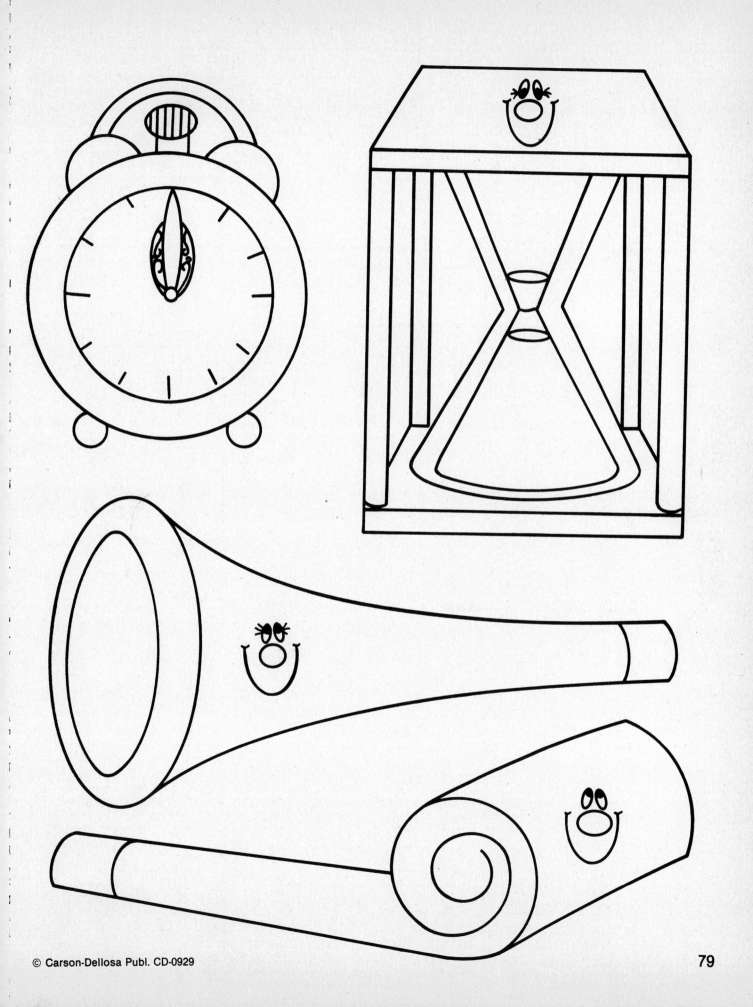

79

80

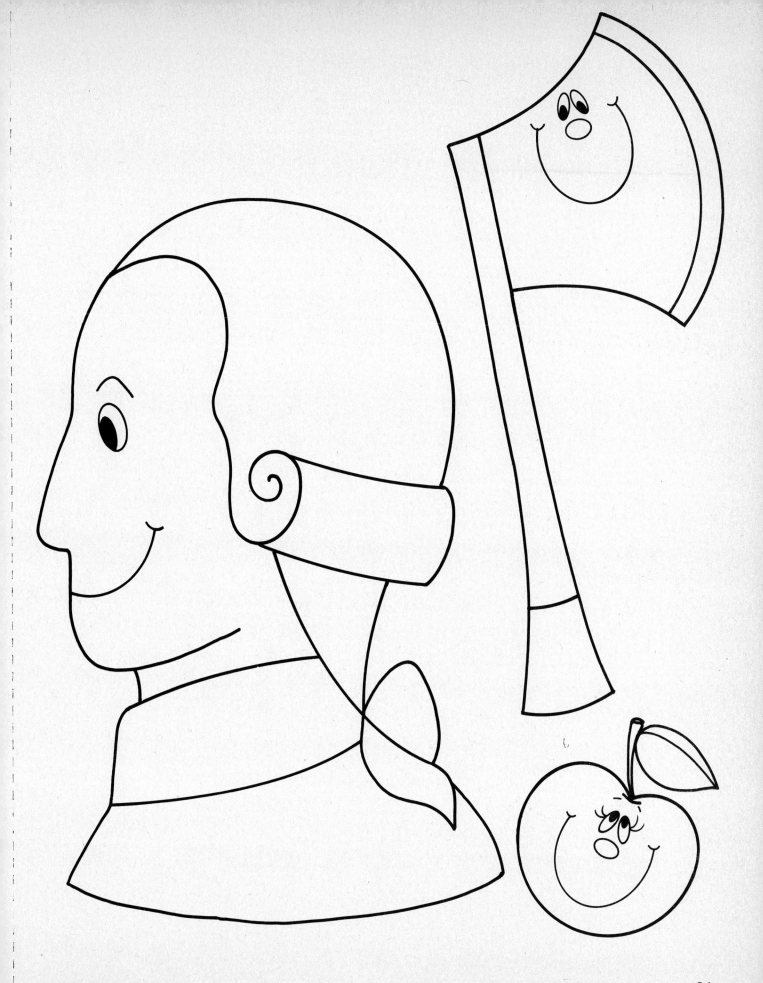

81

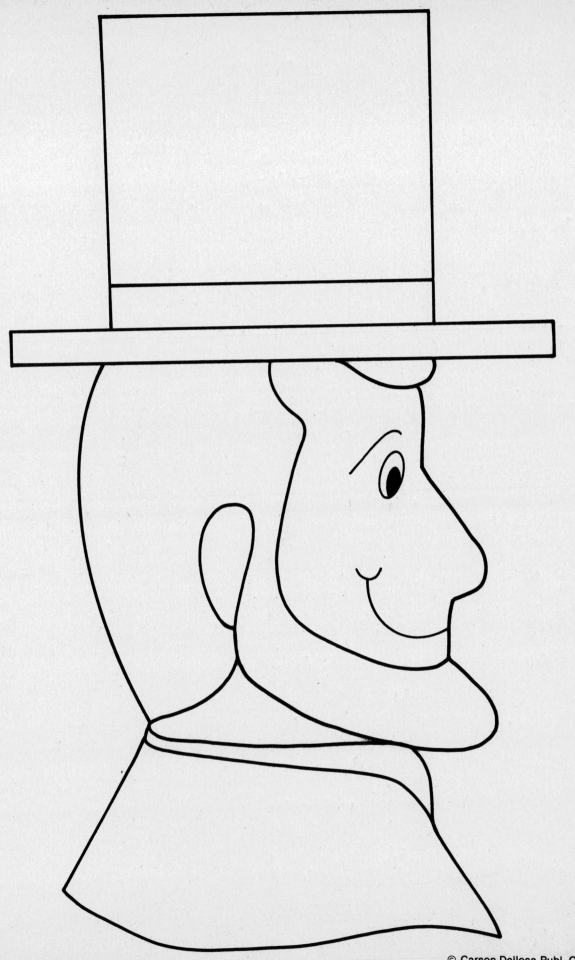

82

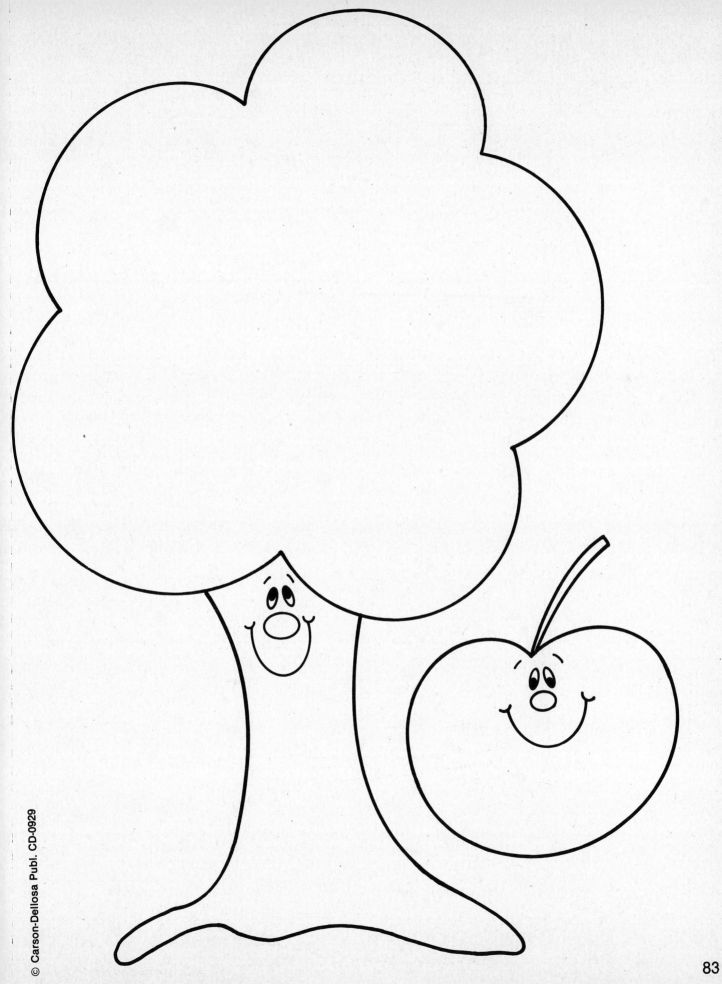

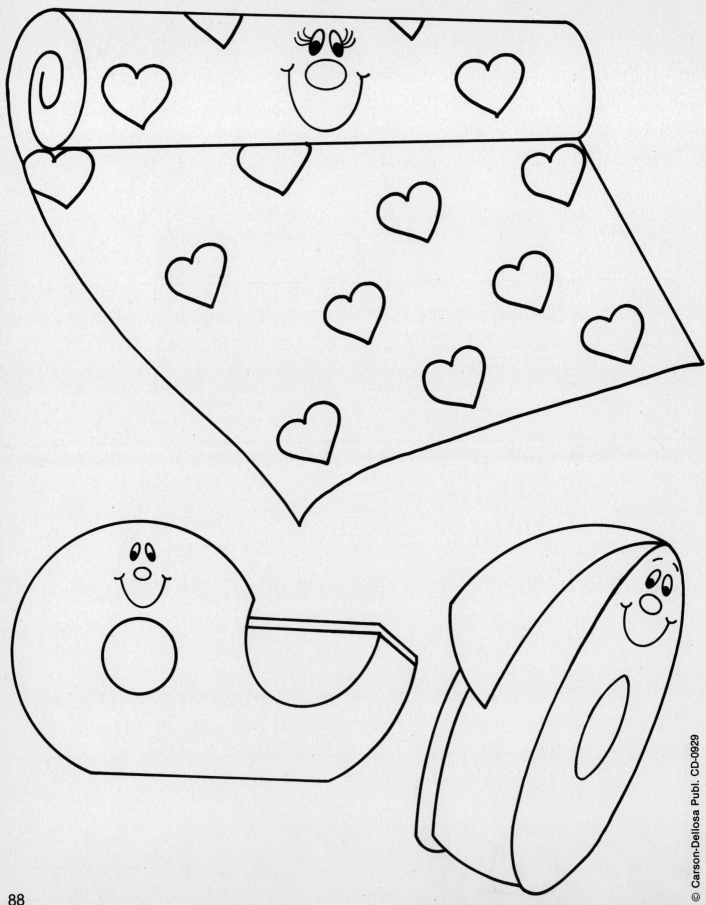

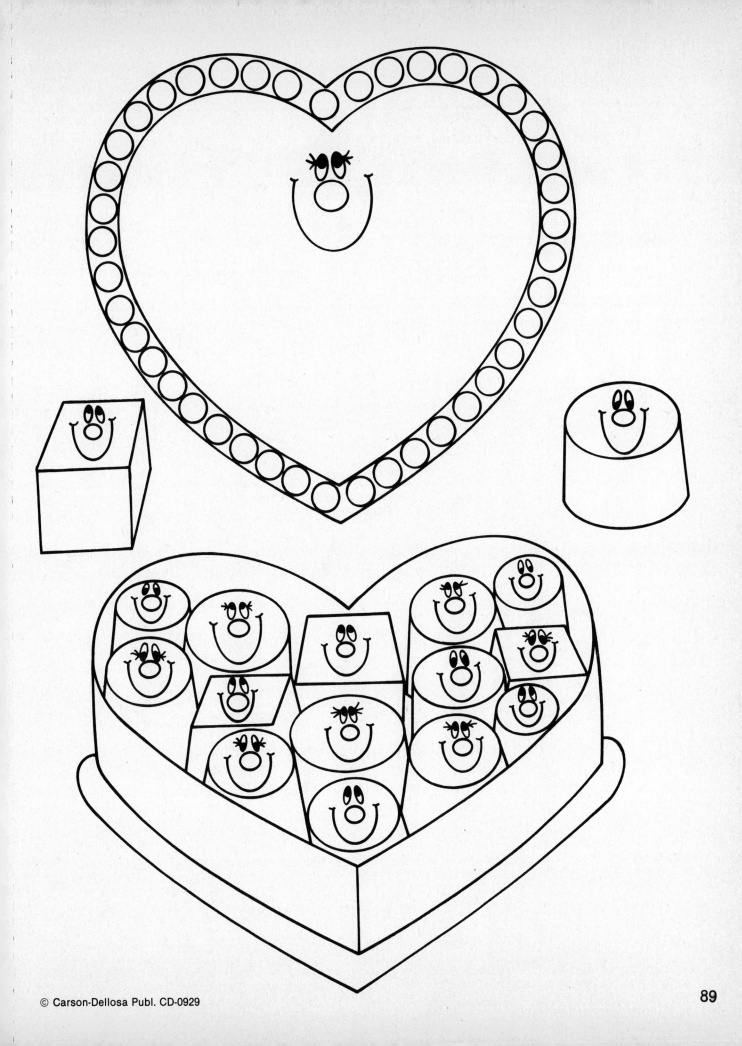

89

90

92

94

96

98

100

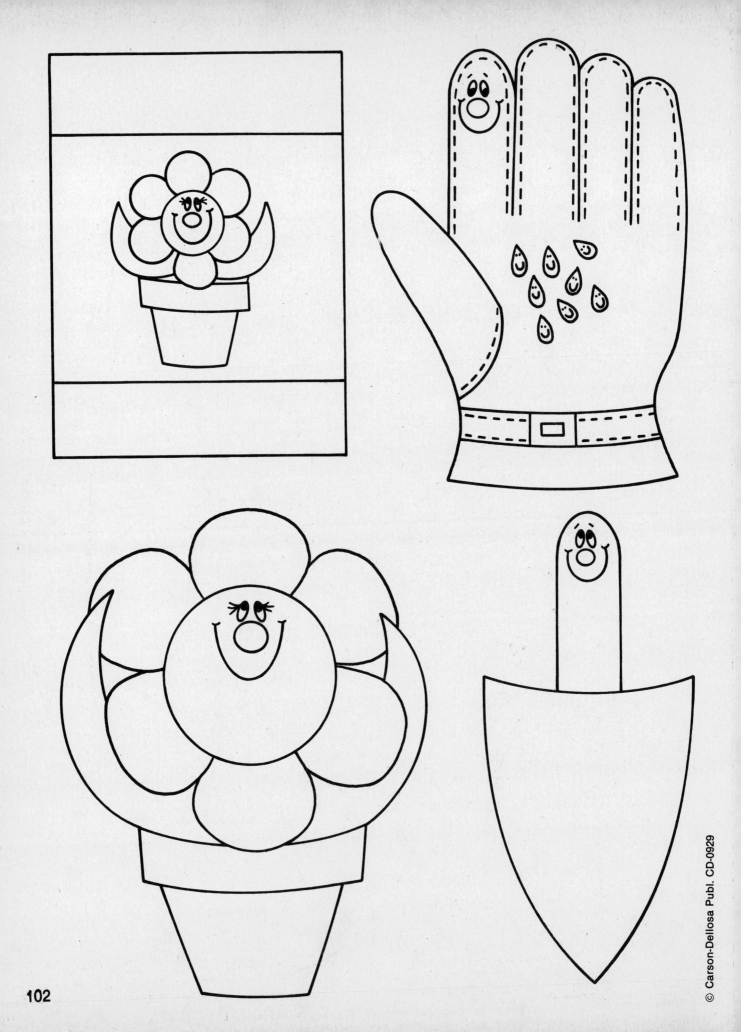

102

104

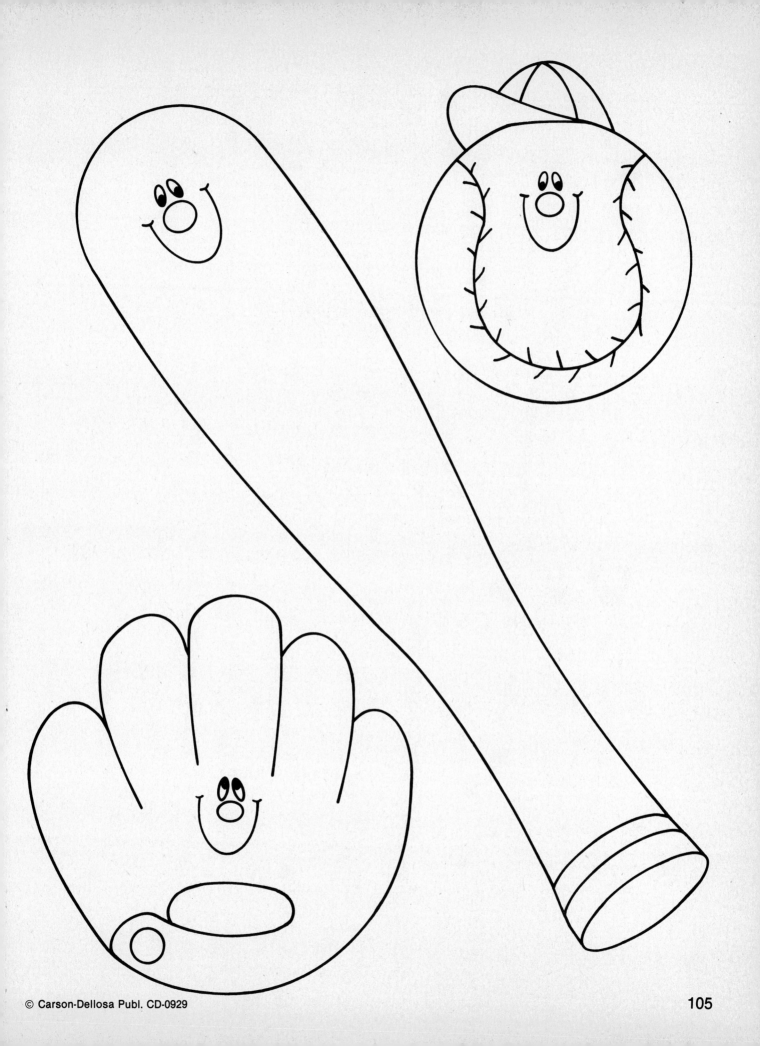

105

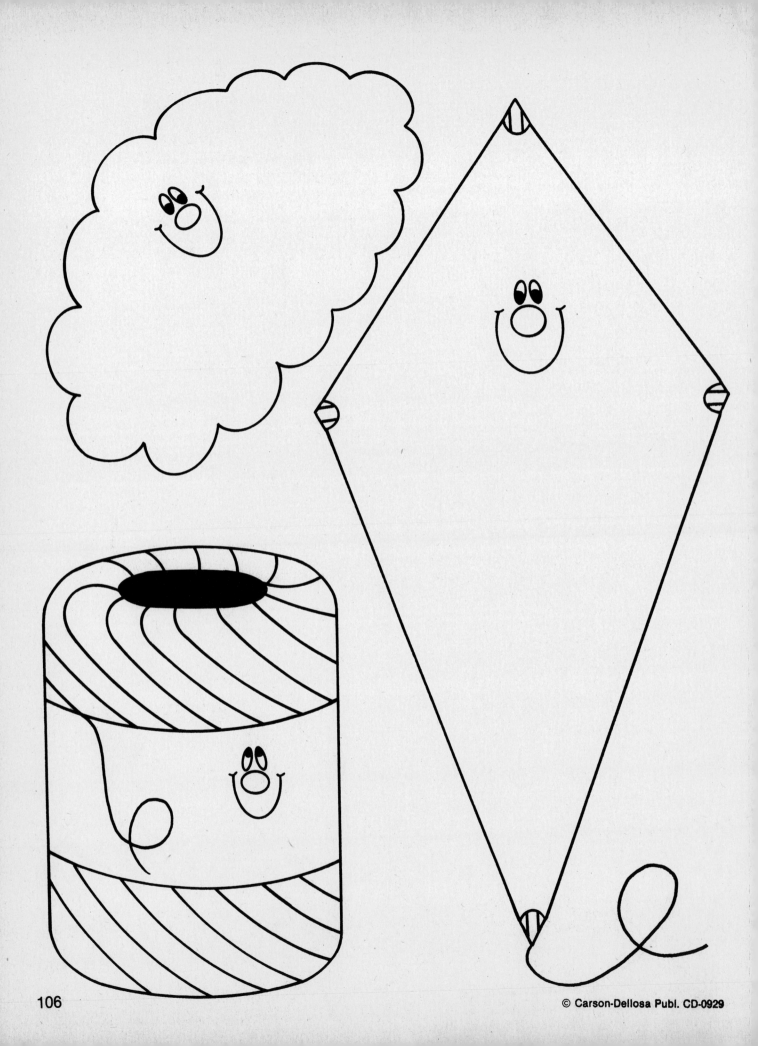

106

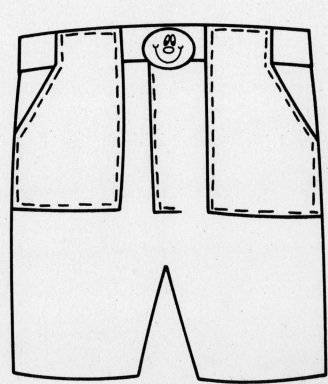

108

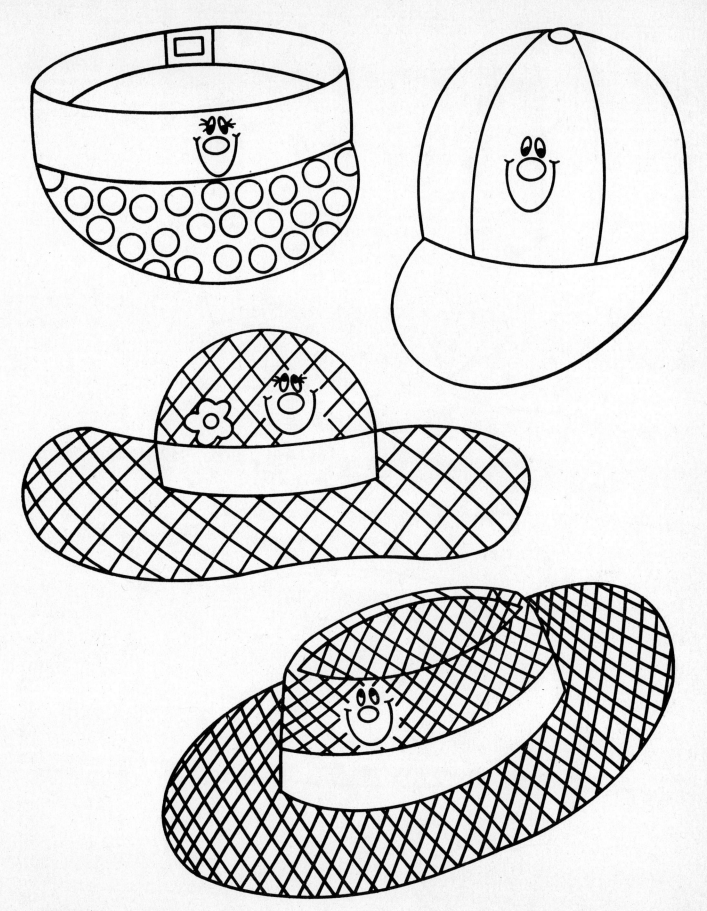

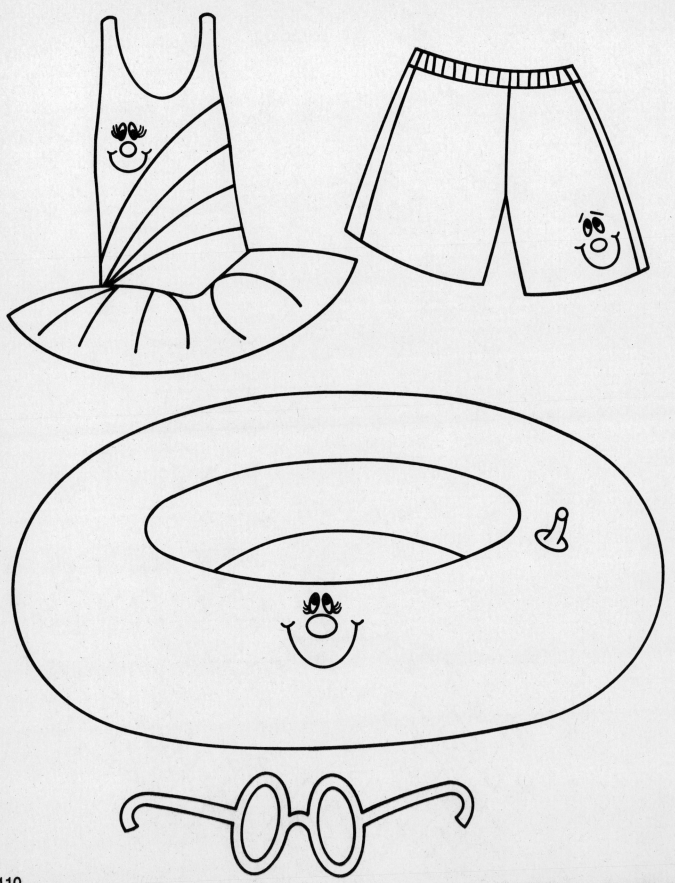

110

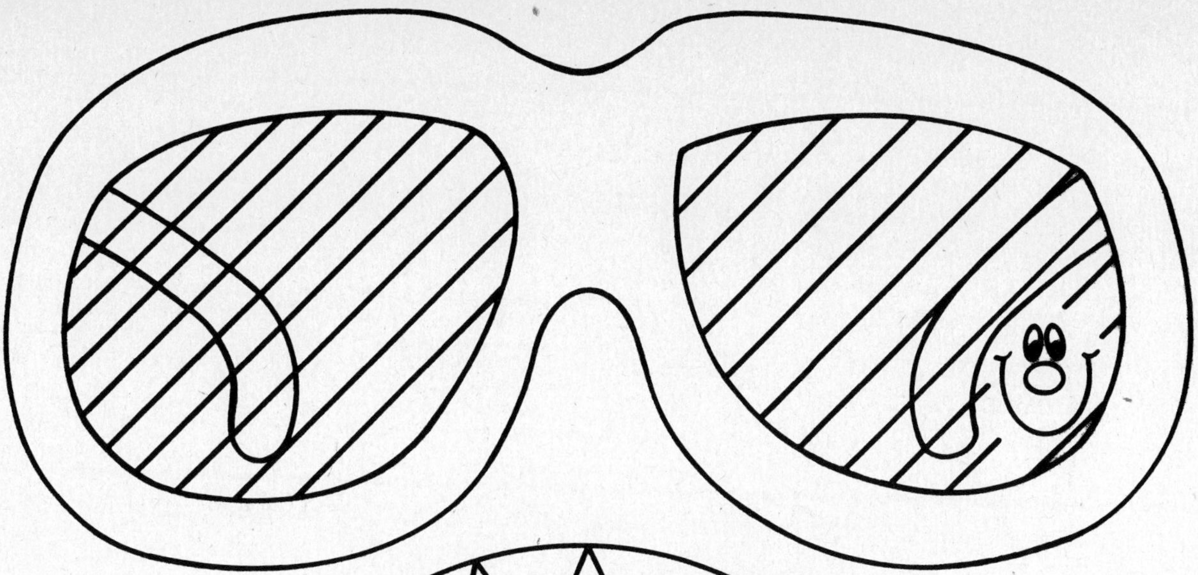

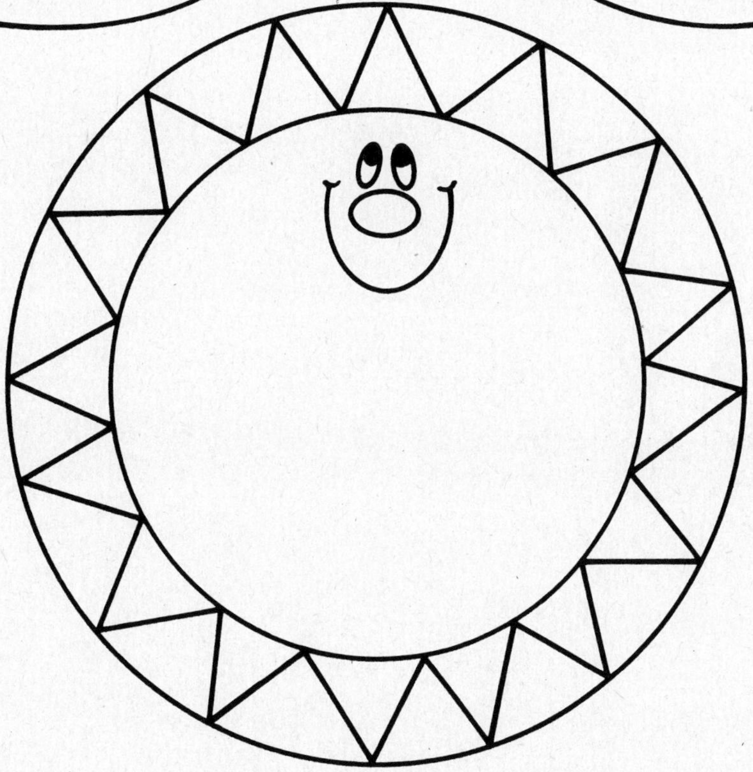

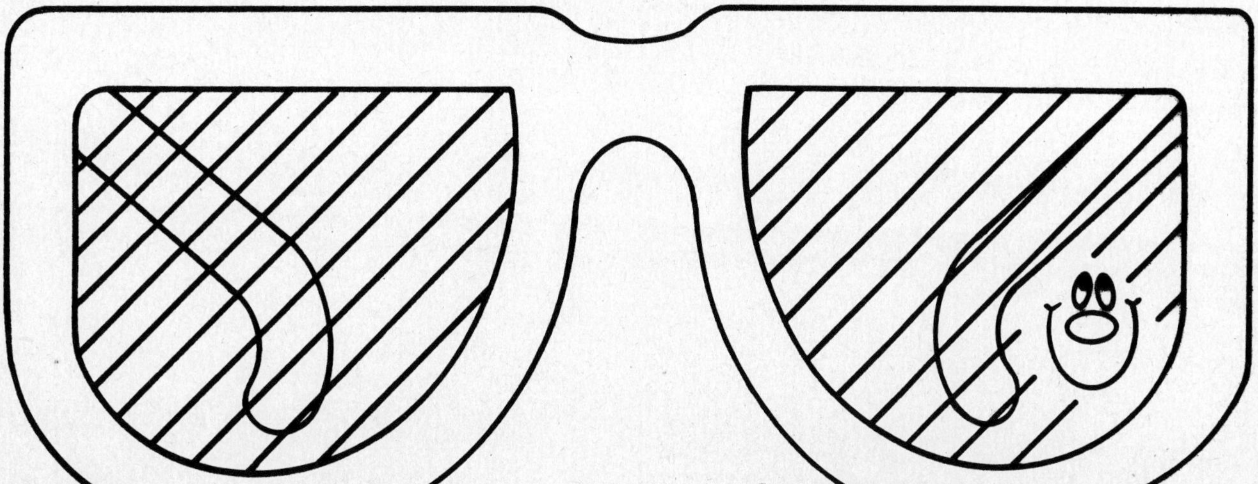

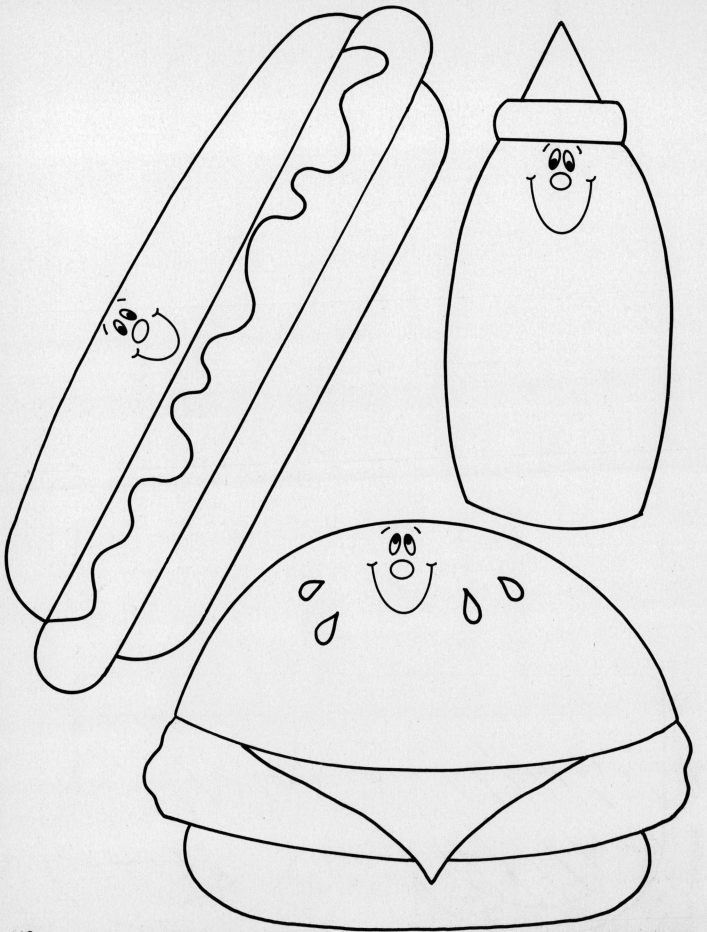

112

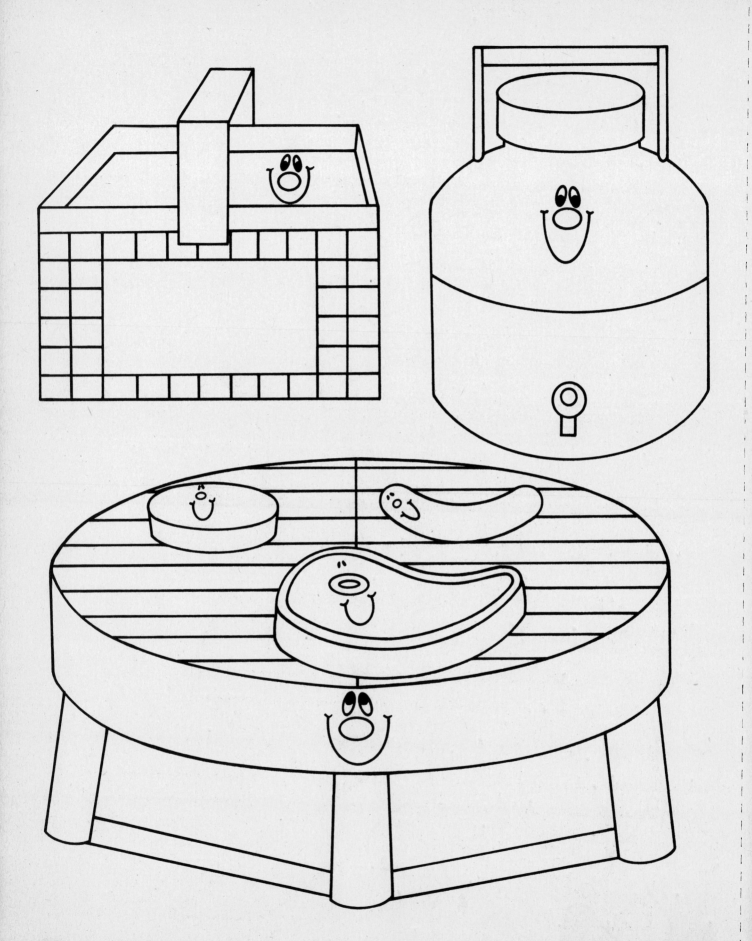

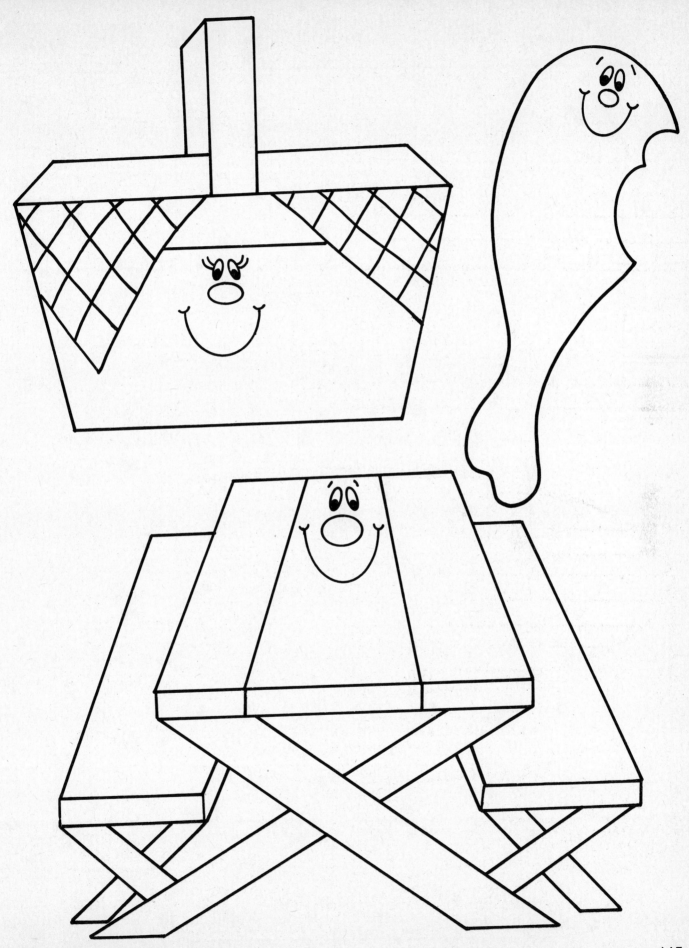

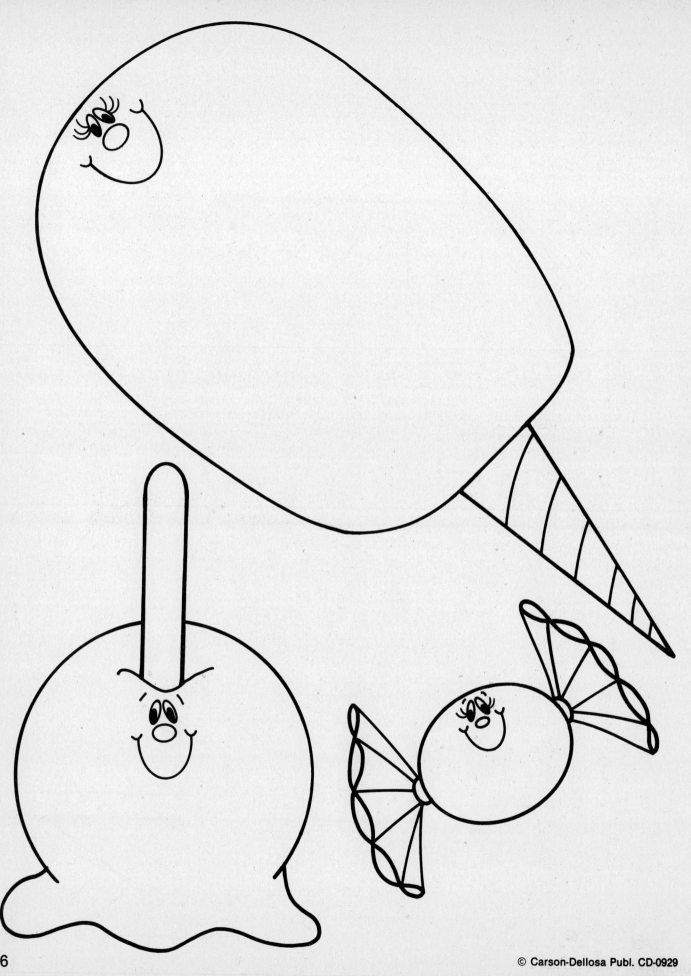

116

117

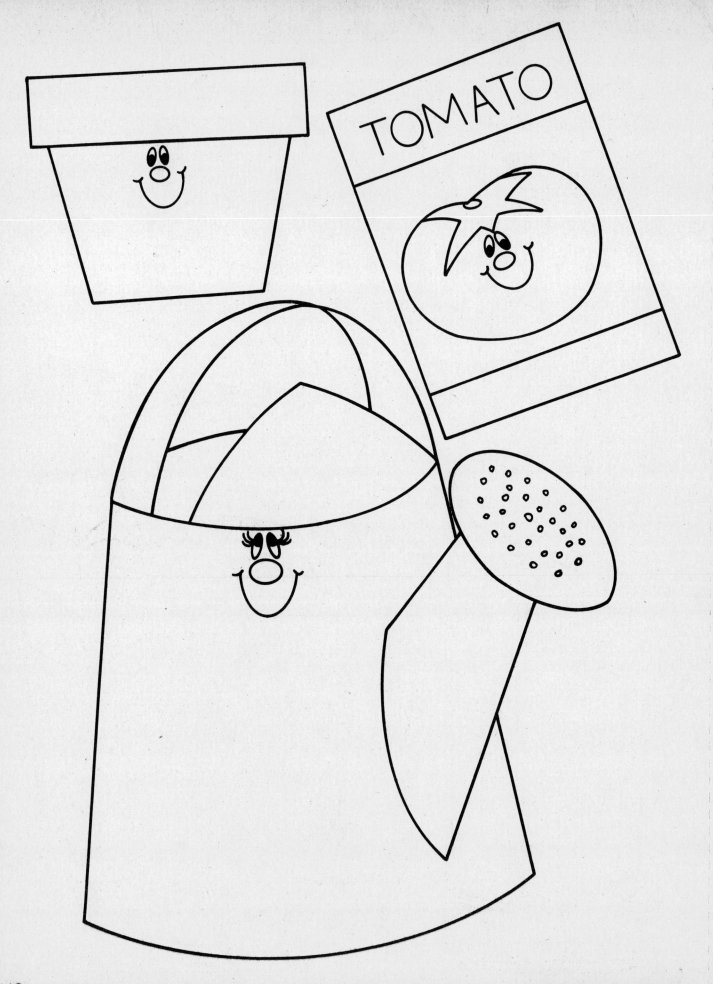

118

120

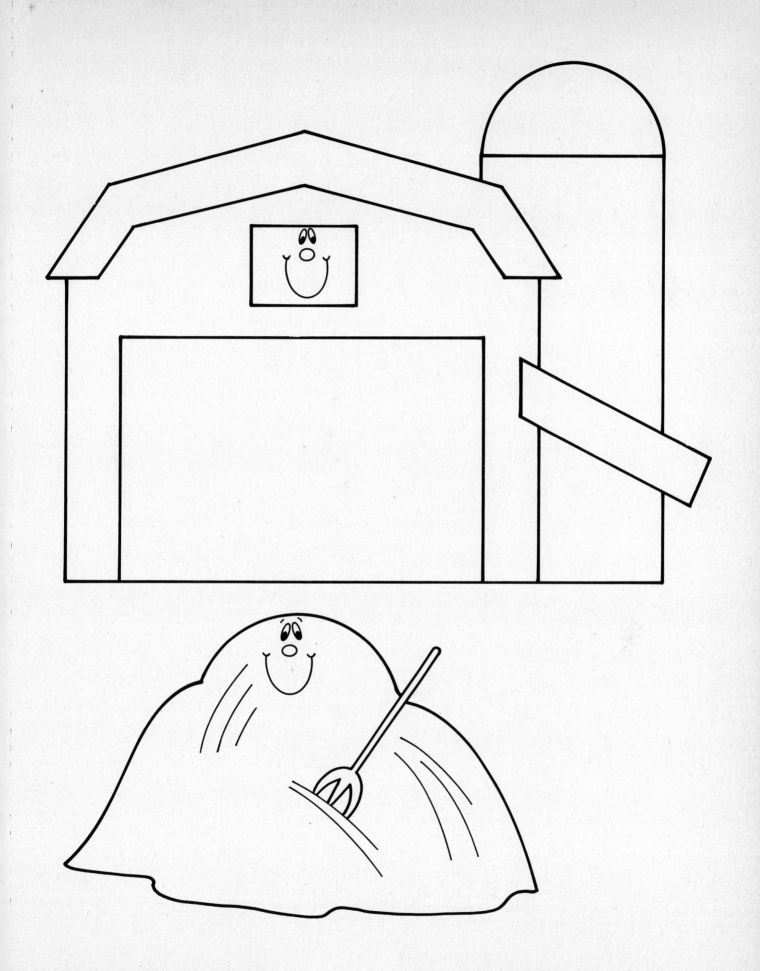

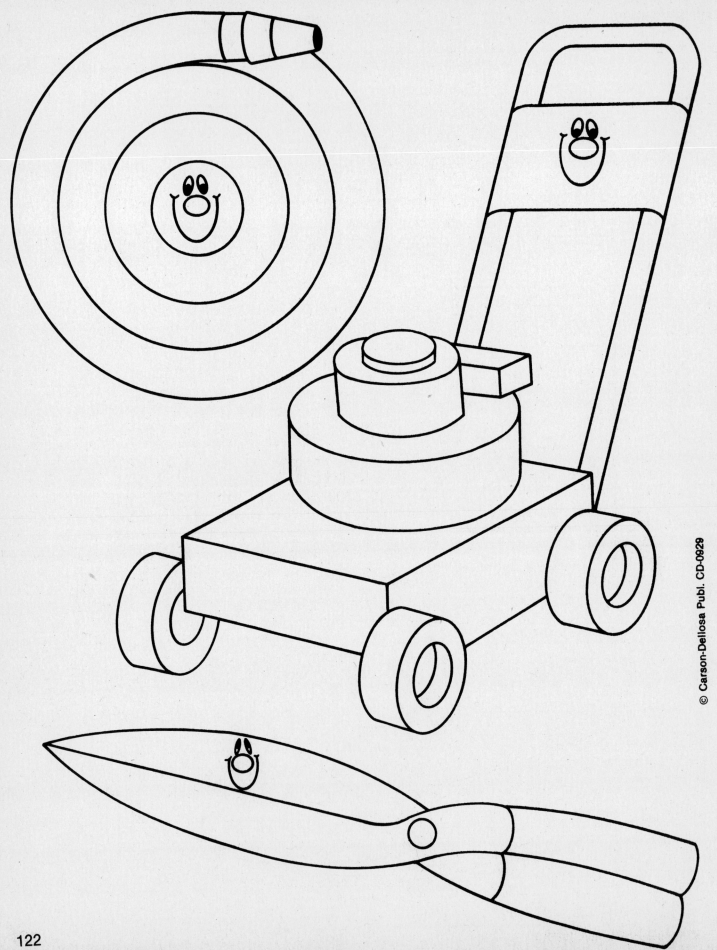

122

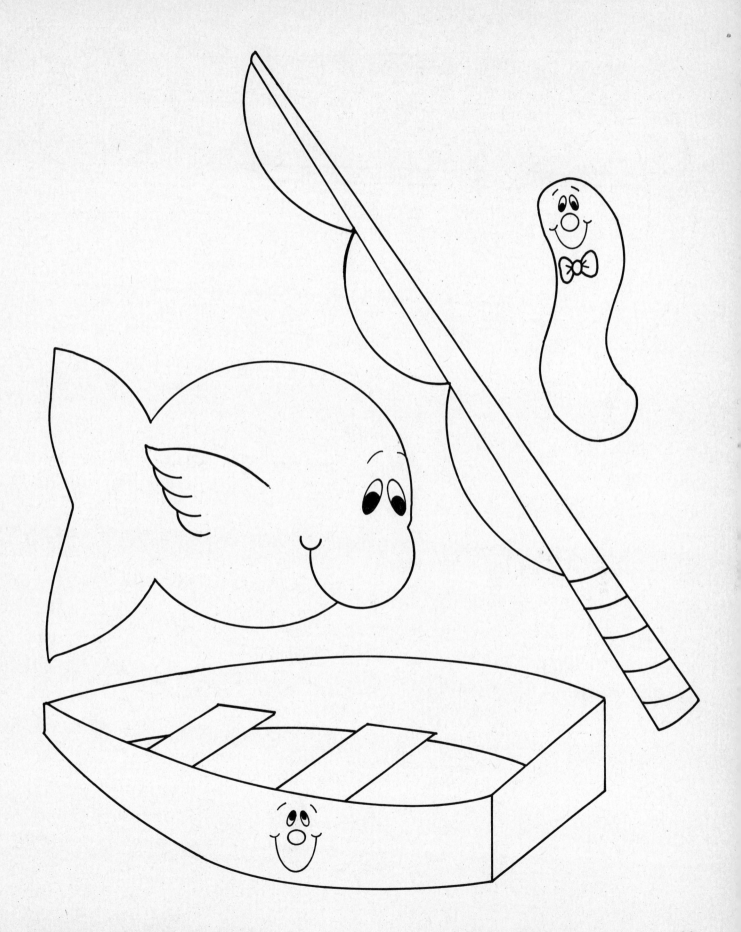

123

124

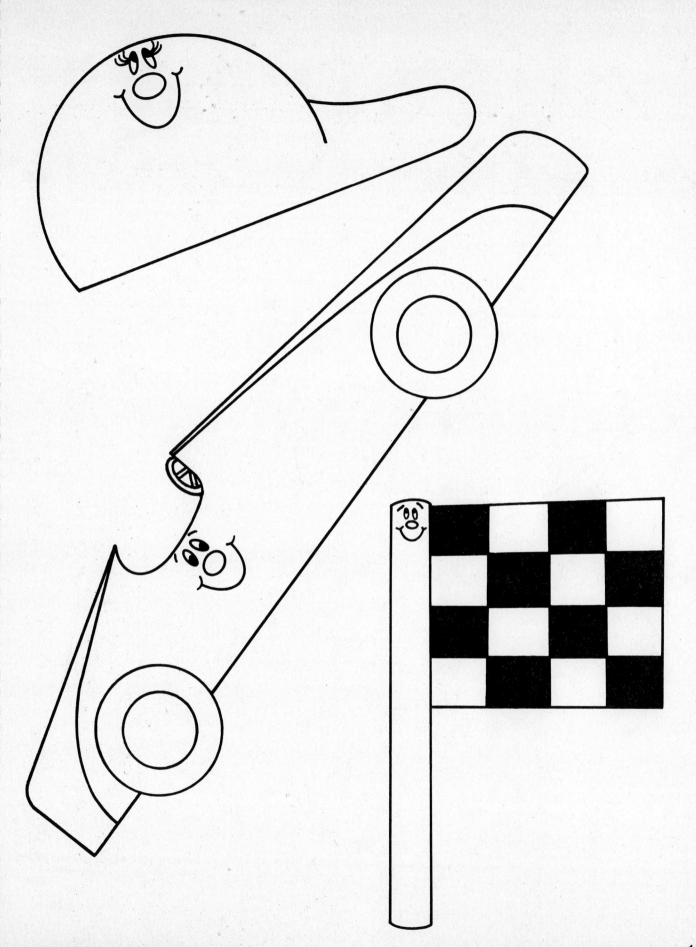

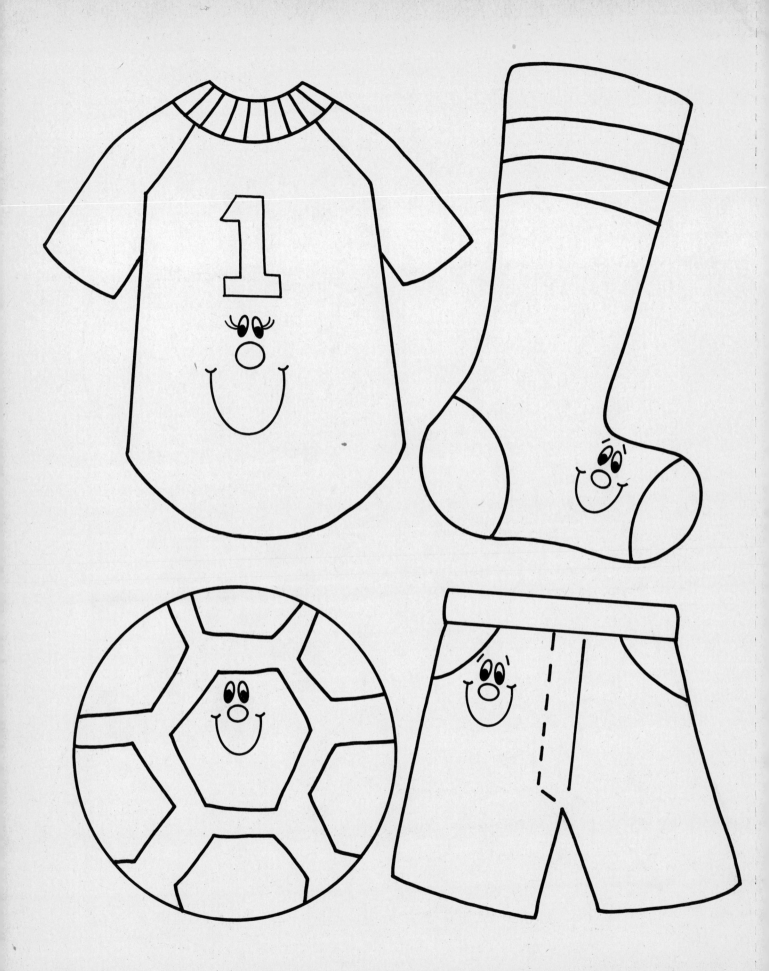

126

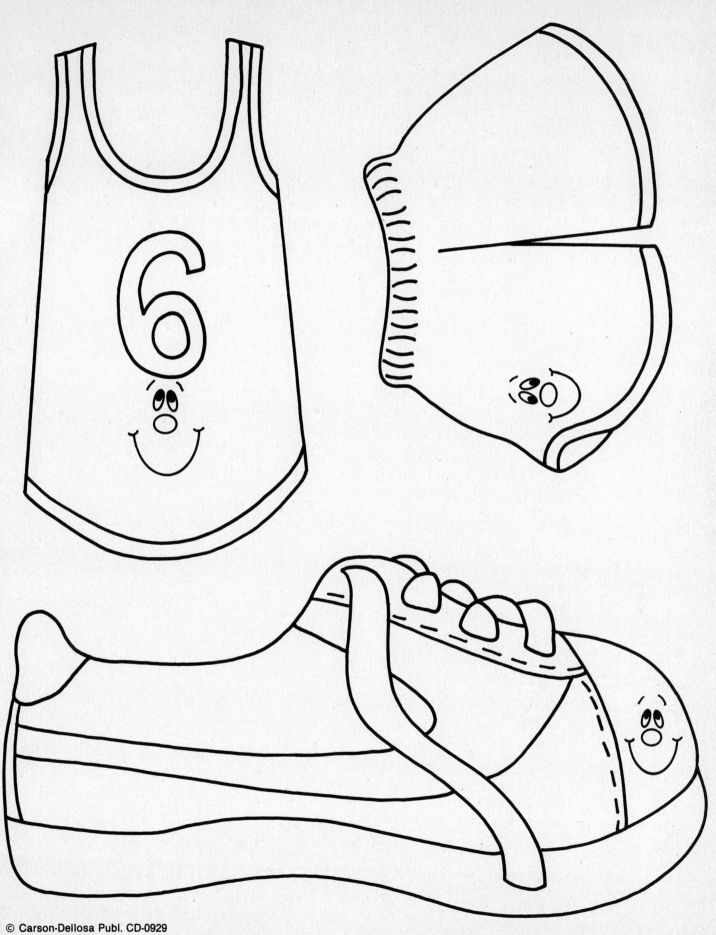

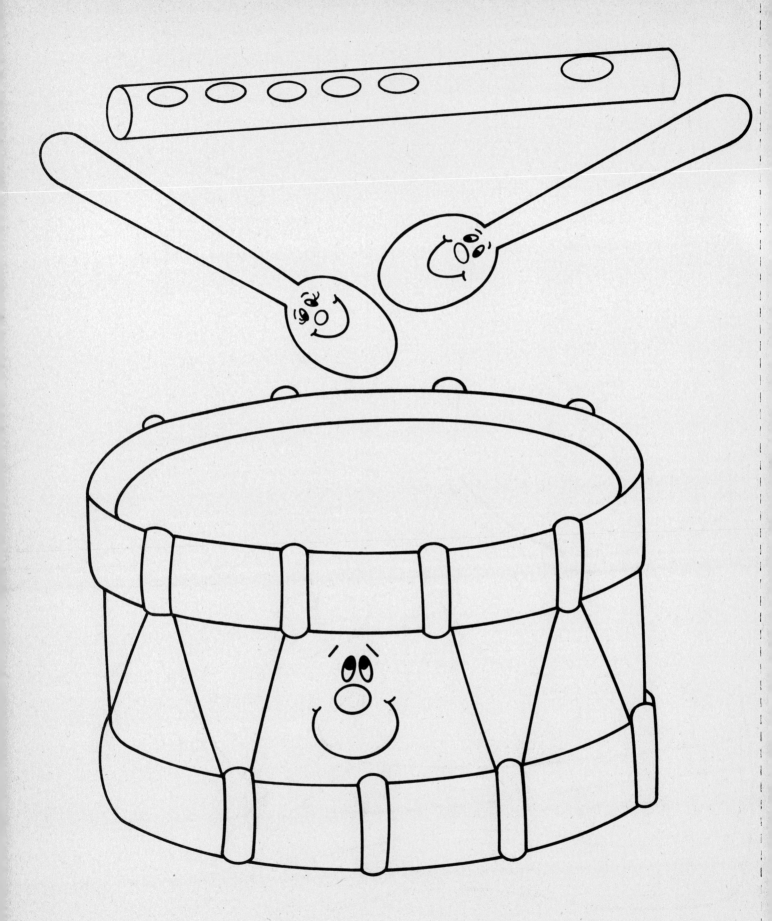

129

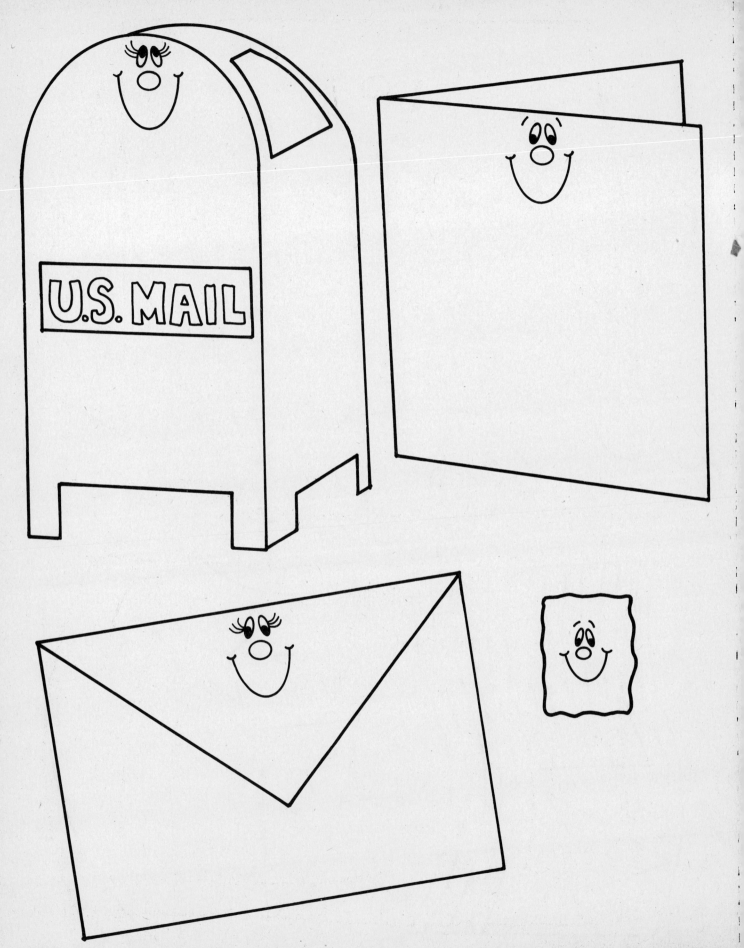

130

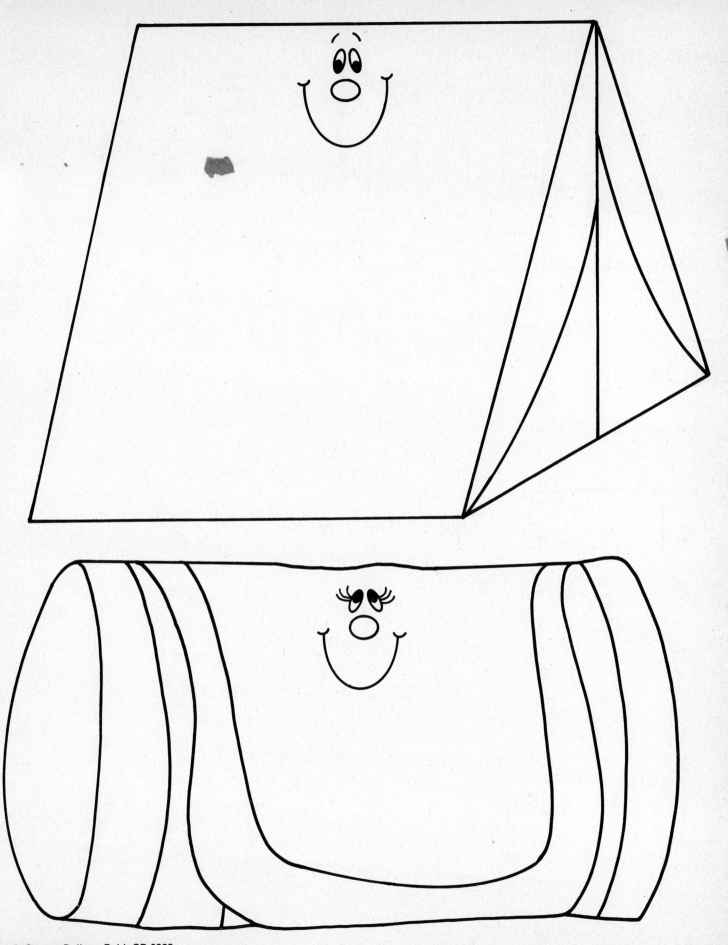

132

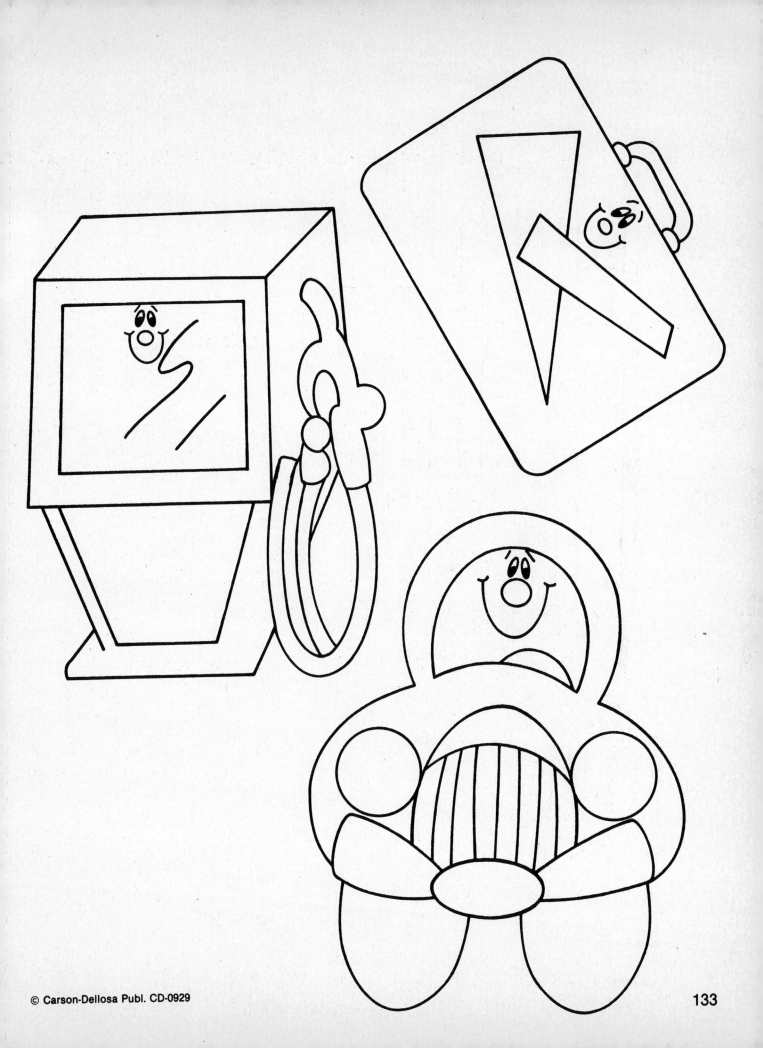

133

134

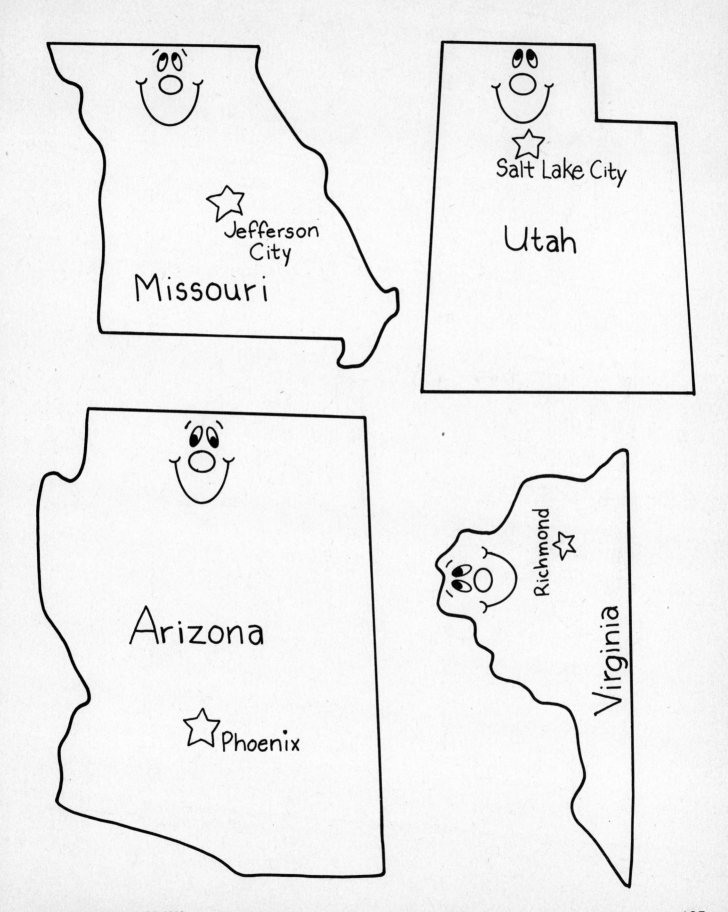

Jefferson
City

Missouri

Salt Lake City

Utah

Arizona

☆ Phoenix

Richmond

Virginia

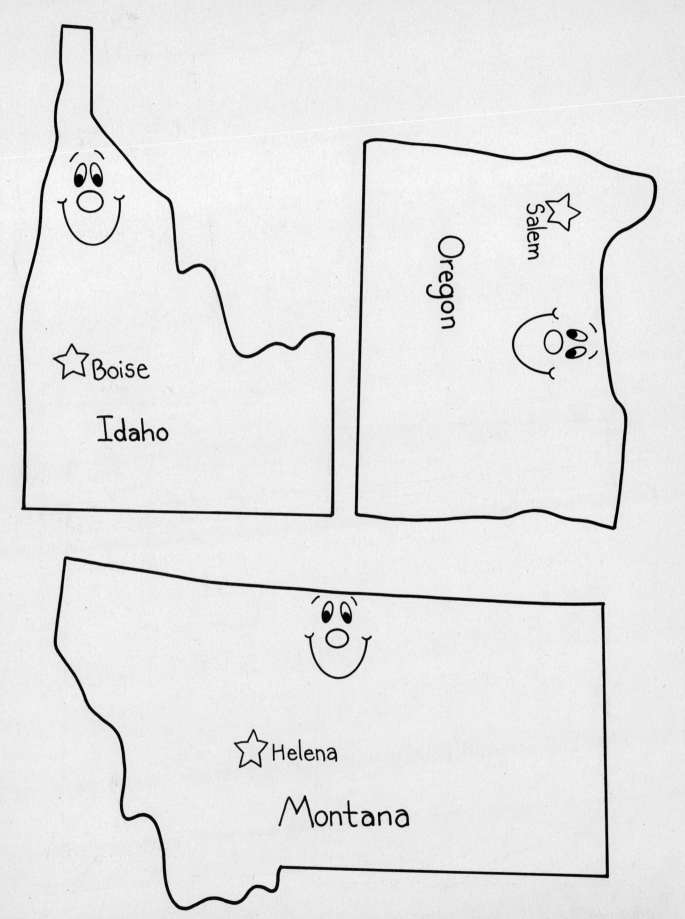

Boise

Idaho

Oregon

Salem

Helena

Montana

136

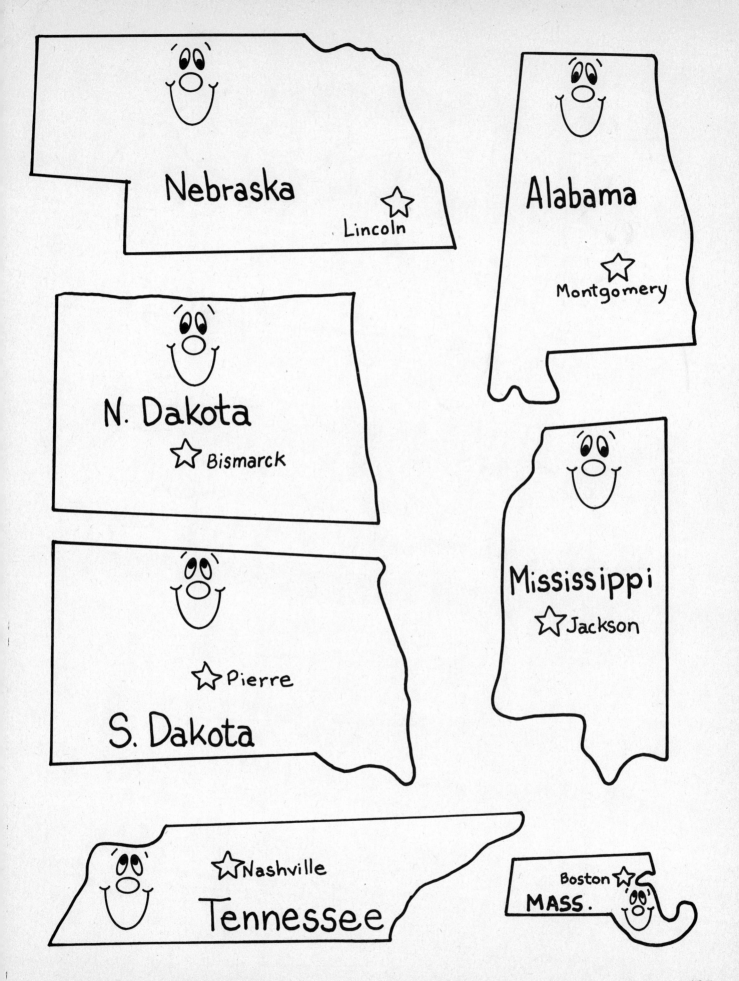

Nebraska

★ Lincoln

Alabama

★ Montgomery

N. Dakota

★ Bismarck

Mississippi

★ Jackson

S. Dakota

★ Pierre

★ Nashville

Tennessee

Boston ★

MASS.

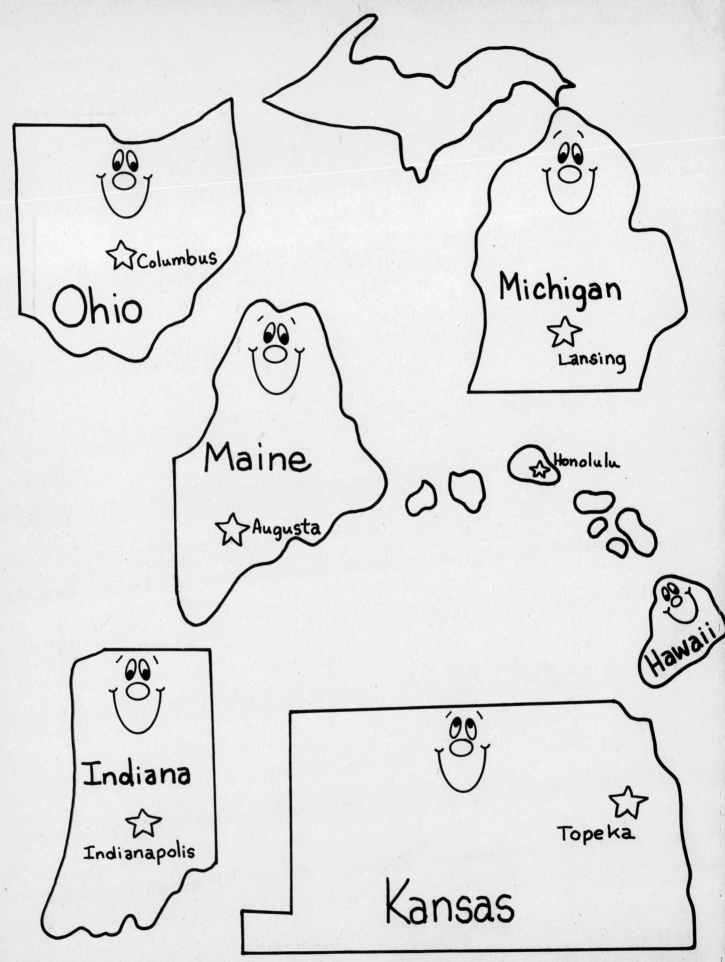

Columbus

Ohio

Michigan

Lansing

Maine

Augusta

Honolulu

Hawaii

Indiana

Indianapolis

Topeka

Kansas

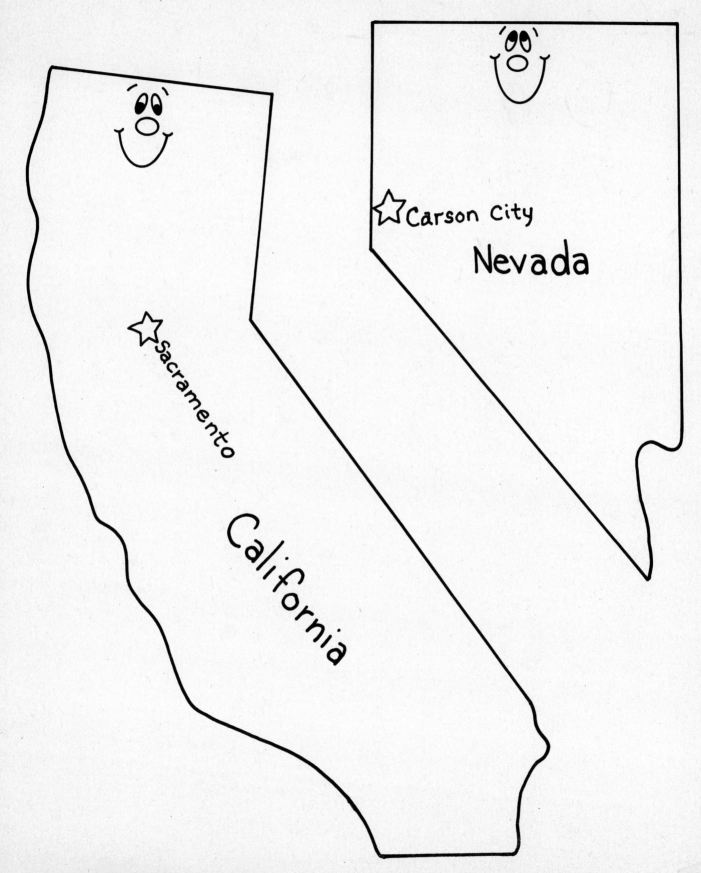

Carson City

Nevada

Sacramento

California

Illinois

☆ Springfield

Alaska

Kentucky

☆ Frankfort

☆ Juneau

Wisconsin

☆ Madison

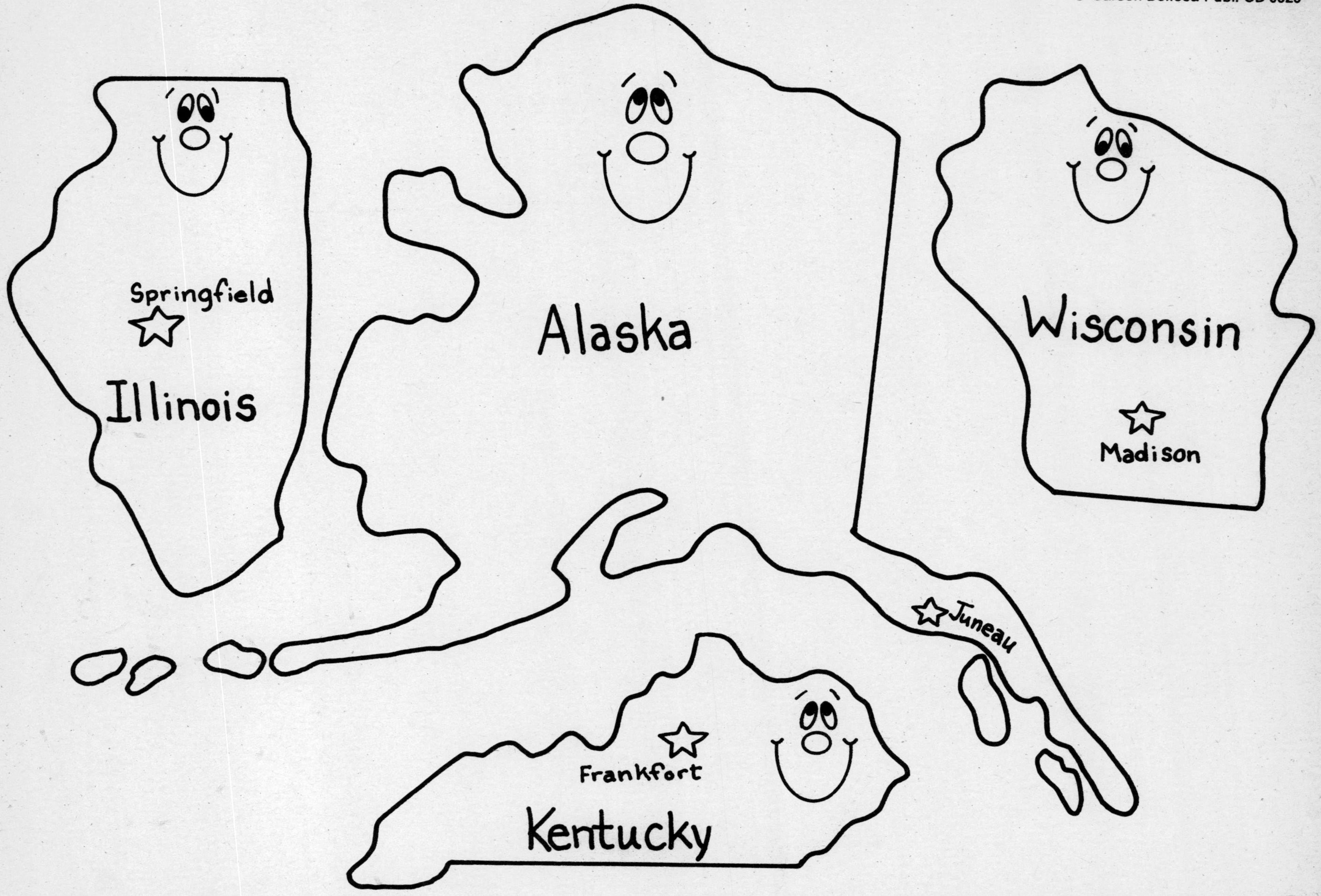

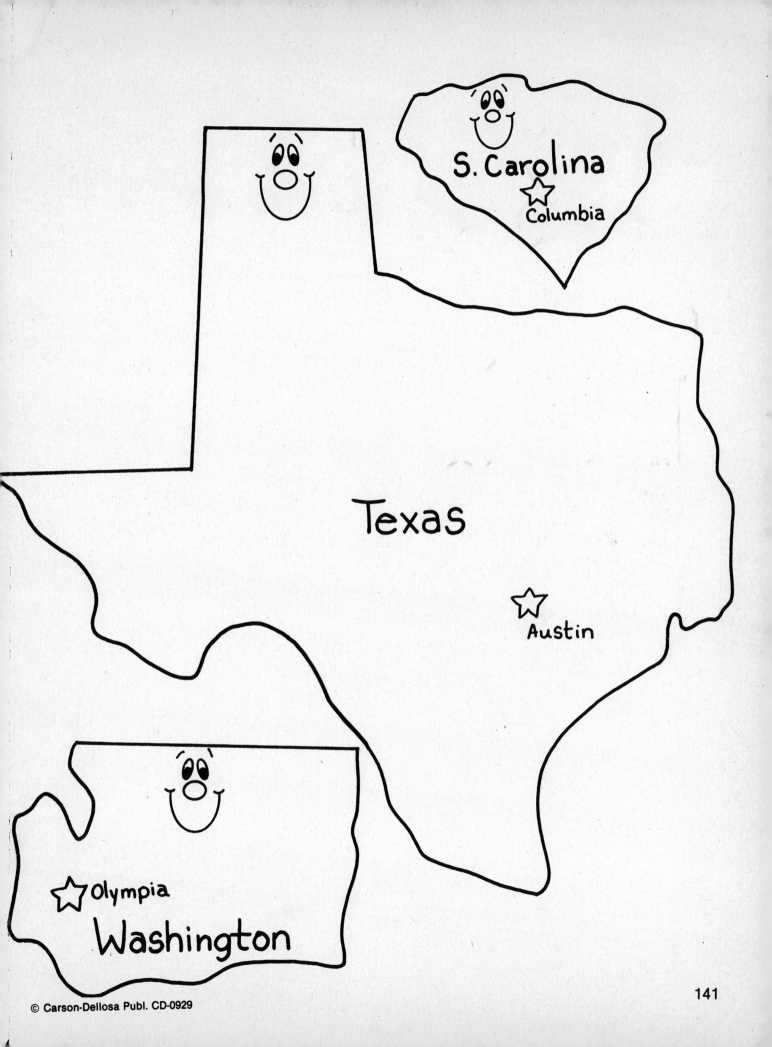

S. Carolina

Columbia

Texas

Austin

Olympia

Washington

Colorado

☆Denver

Wyoming

Cheyenne ☆

☆Santa Fe

New Mexico

Oklahoma

☆ Oklahoma City

142

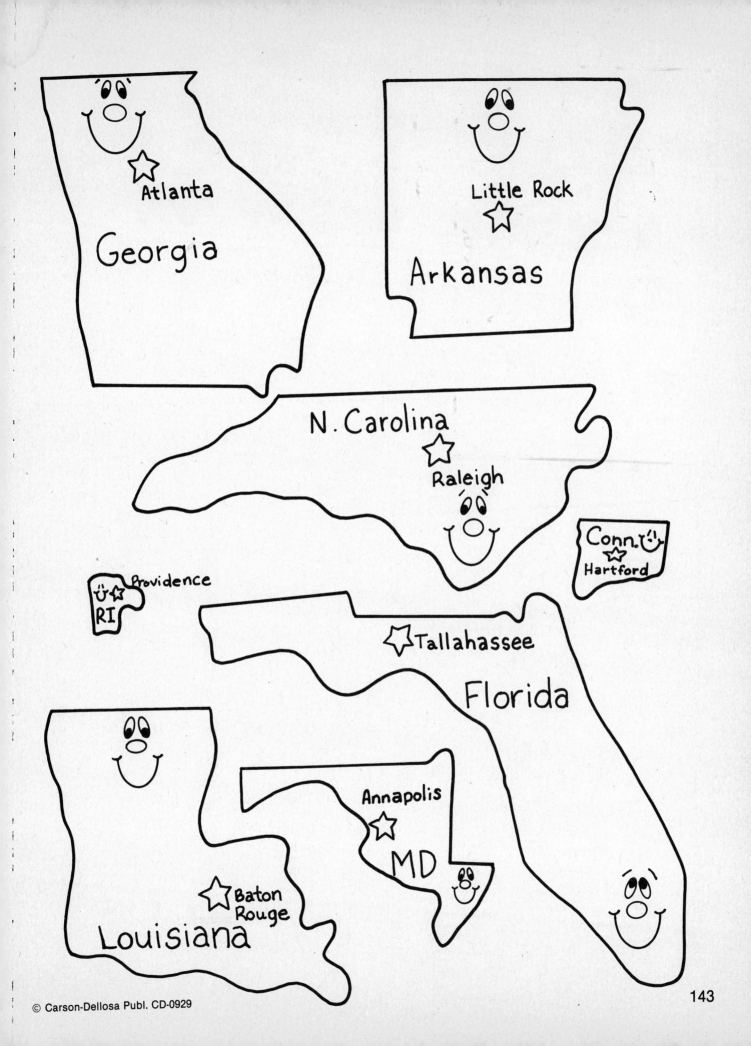

Atlanta

Georgia

Little Rock

Arkansas

N. Carolina

Raleigh

Conn.
Hartford

Providence

RI

Tallahassee

Florida

Annapolis

MD

Baton
Rouge

Louisiana

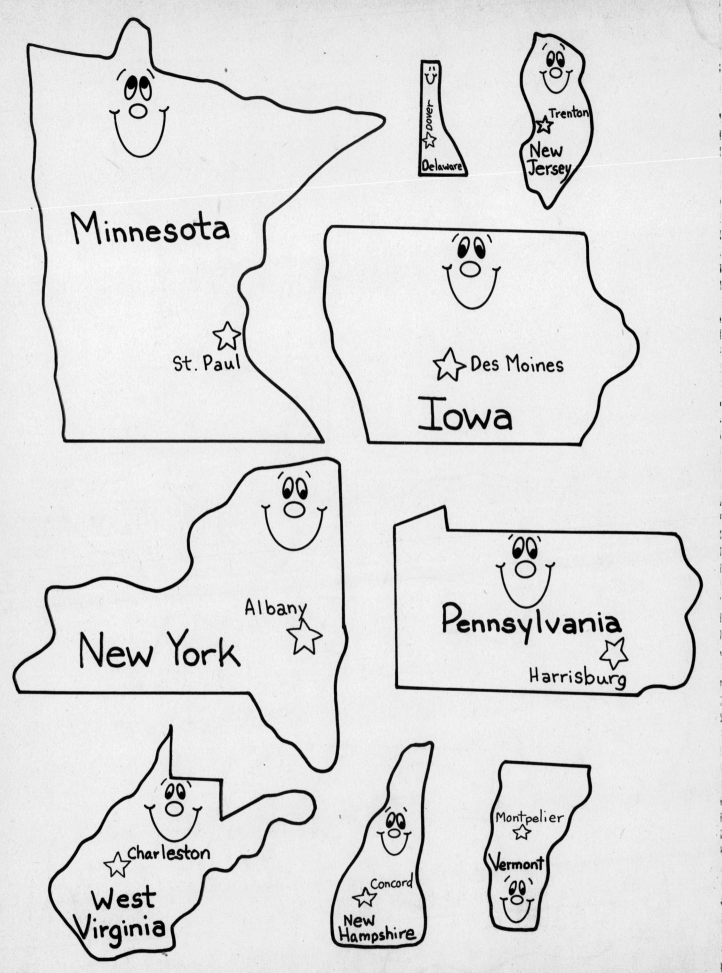

Minnesota

St. Paul

Delaware

Dover

New Jersey

Trenton

Iowa

Des Moines

New York

Albany

Pennsylvania

Harrisburg

West Virginia

Charleston

New Hampshire

Concord

Vermont

Montpelier

144

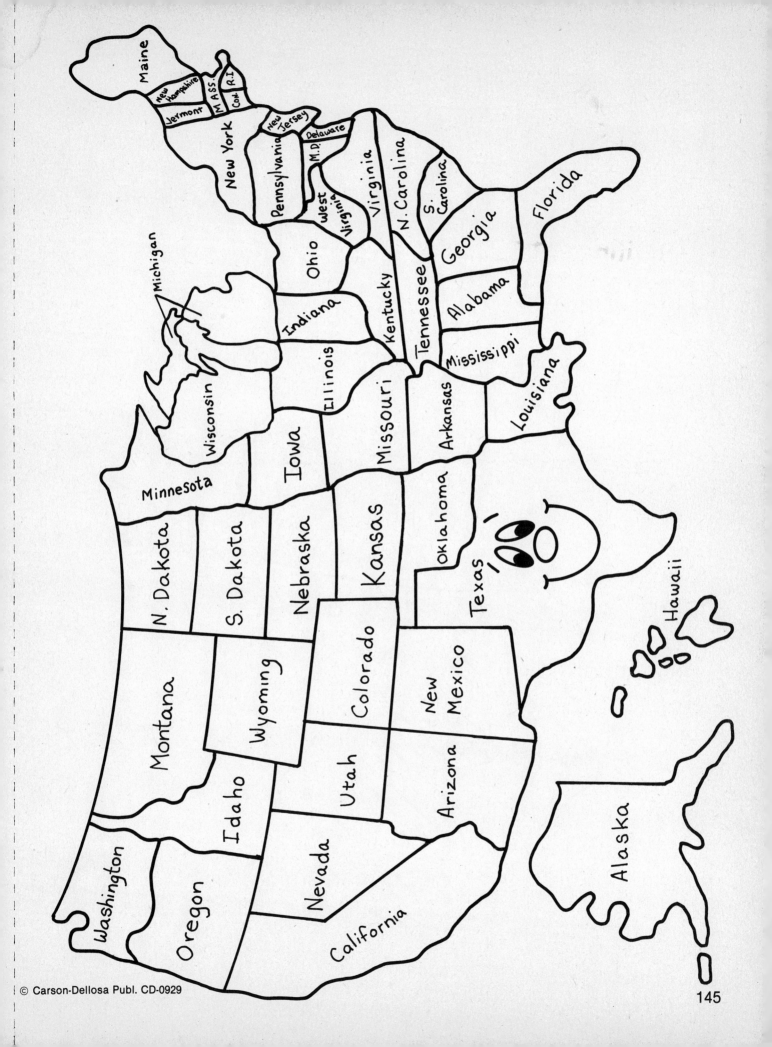

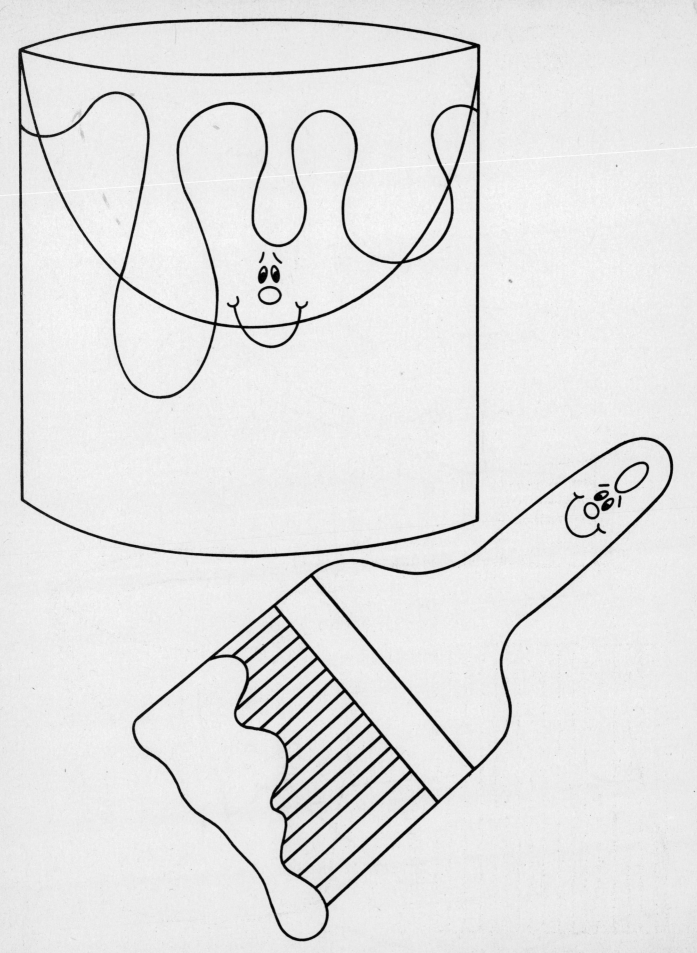

146

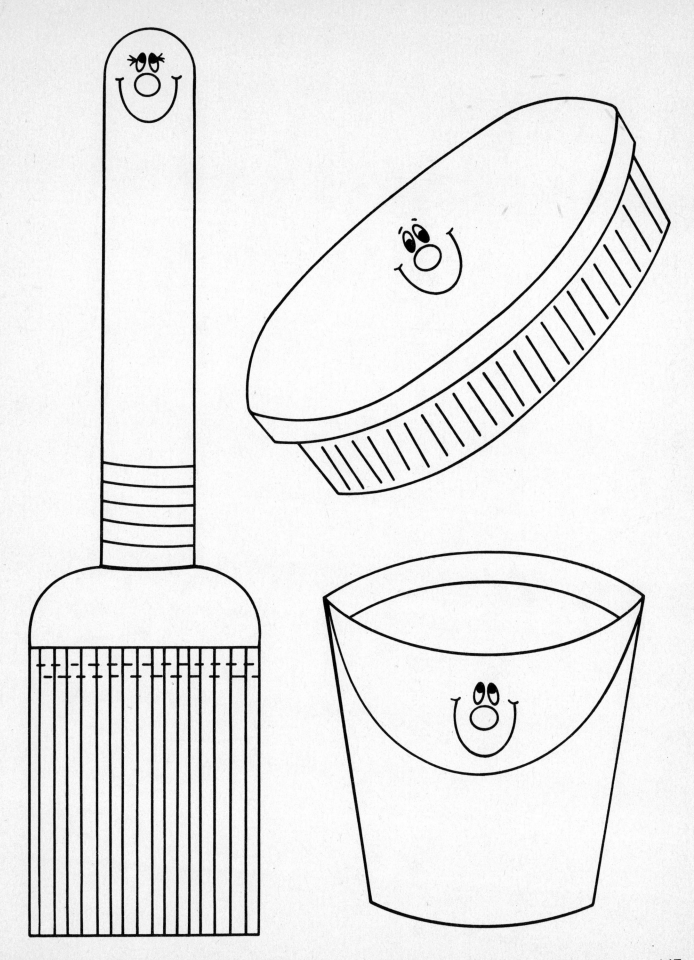

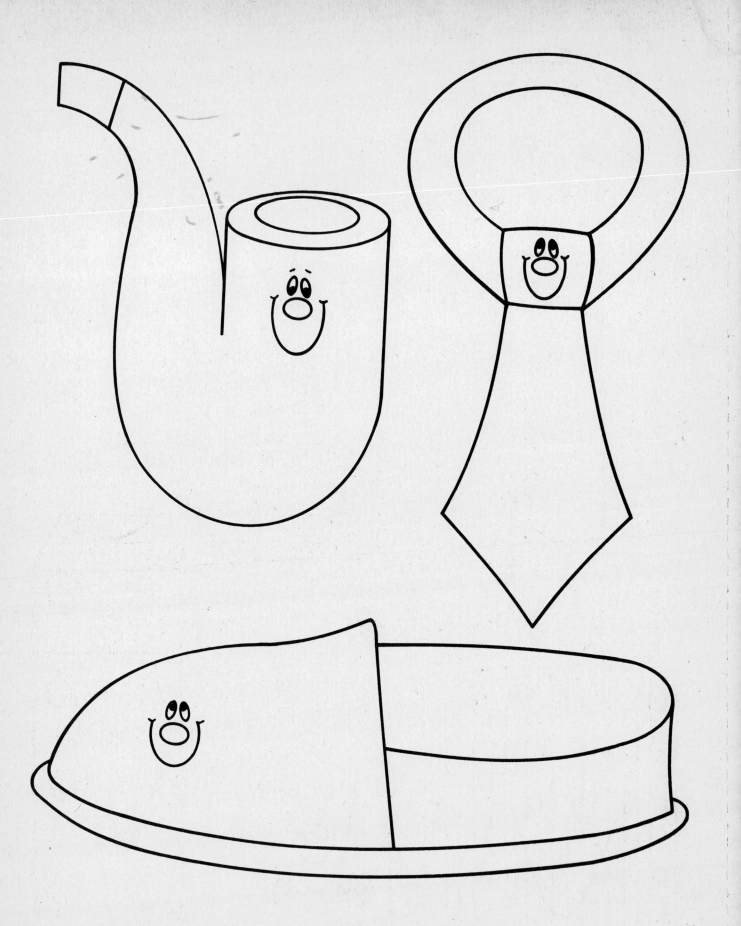

148

149

150

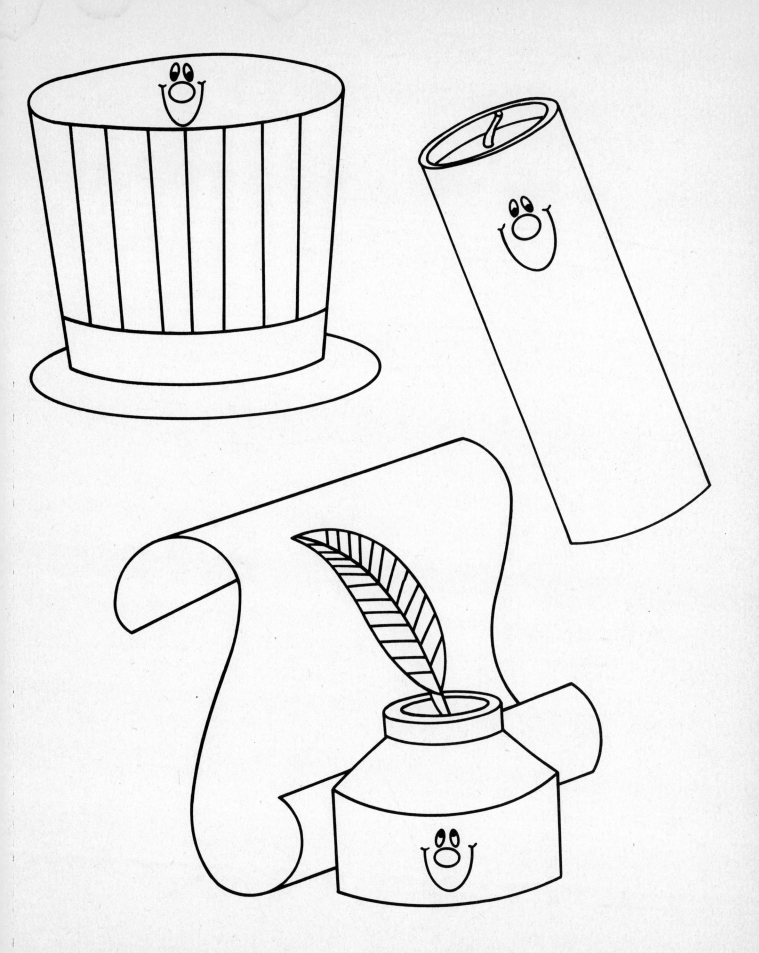

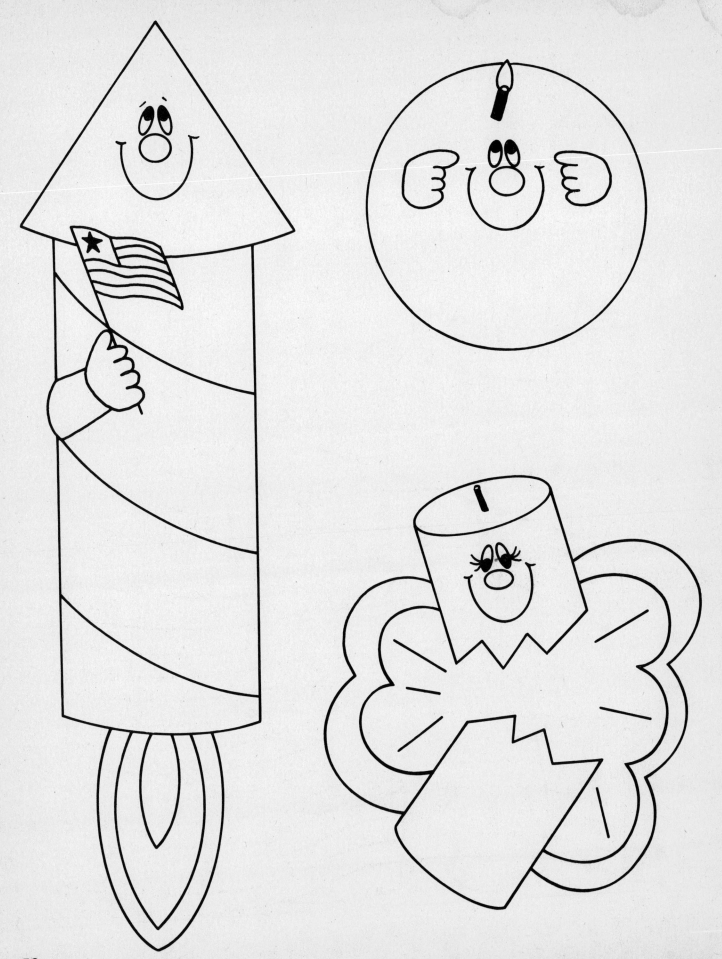

152

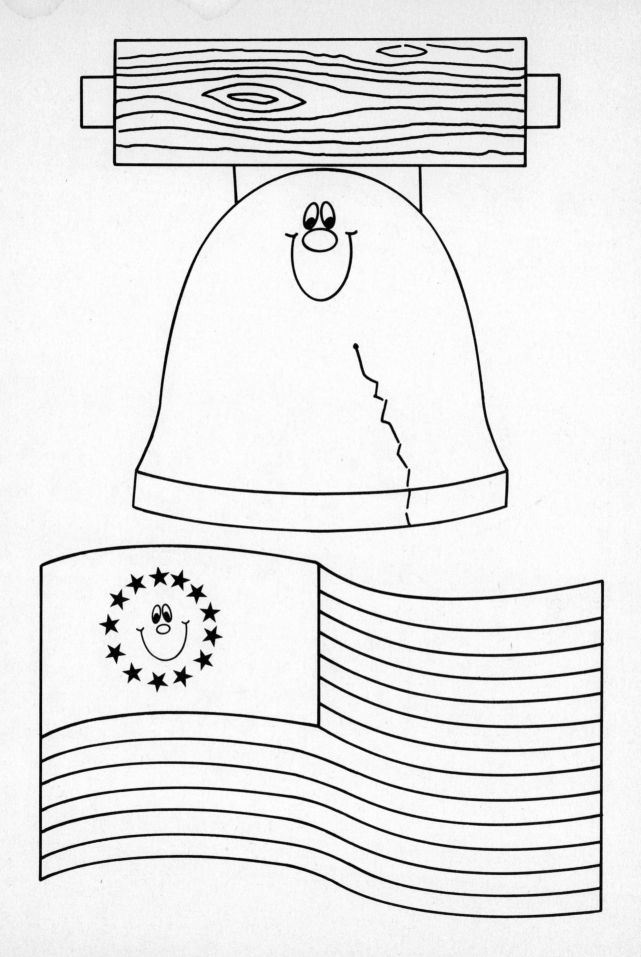

154

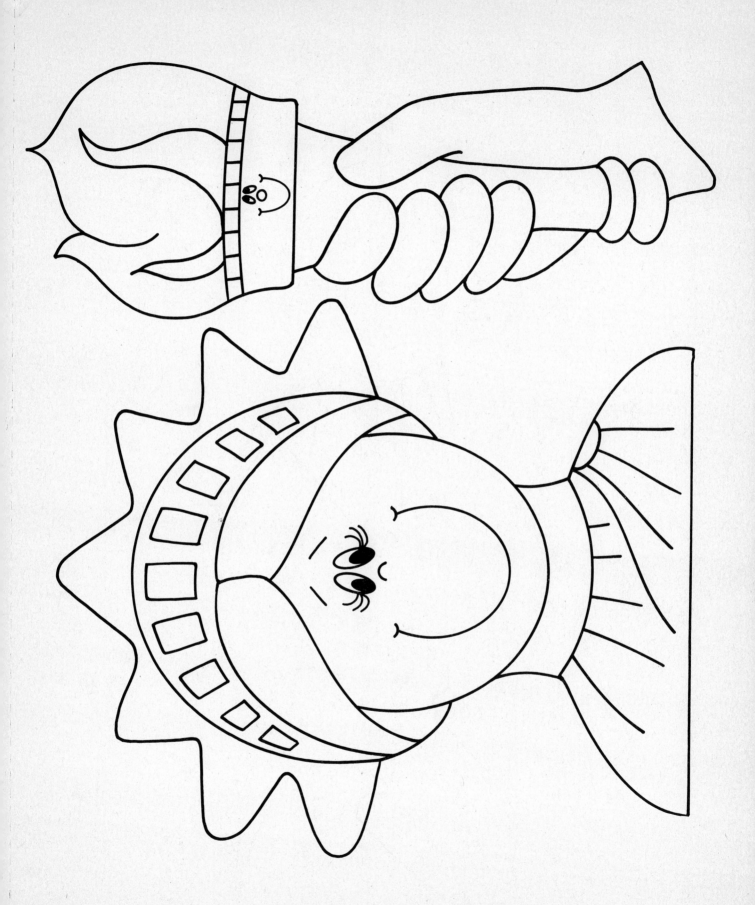

156

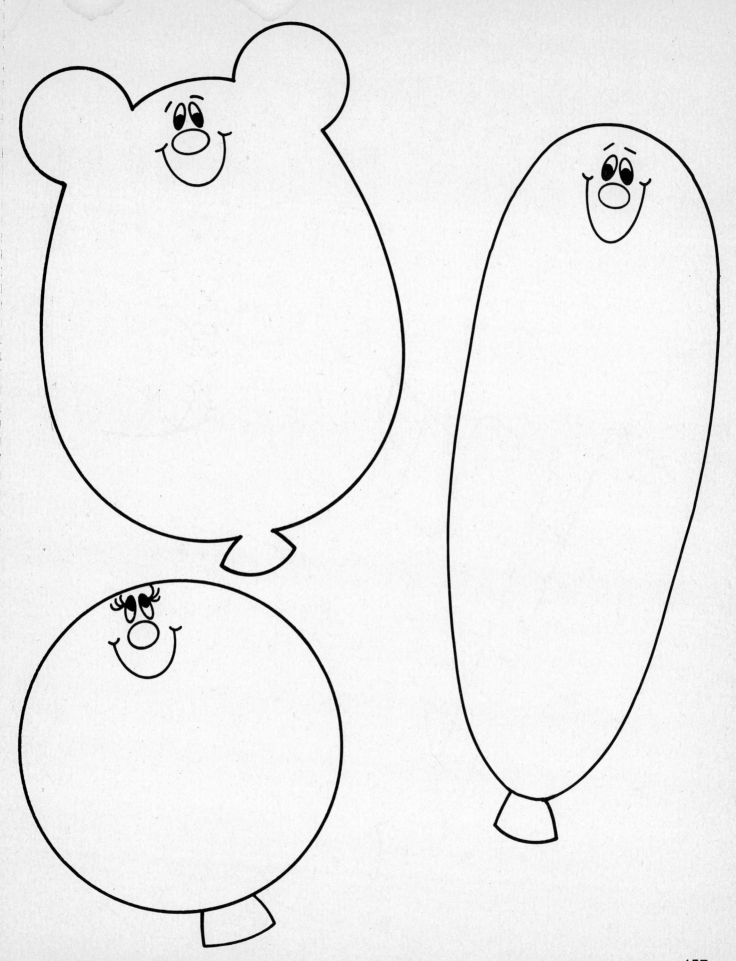

158

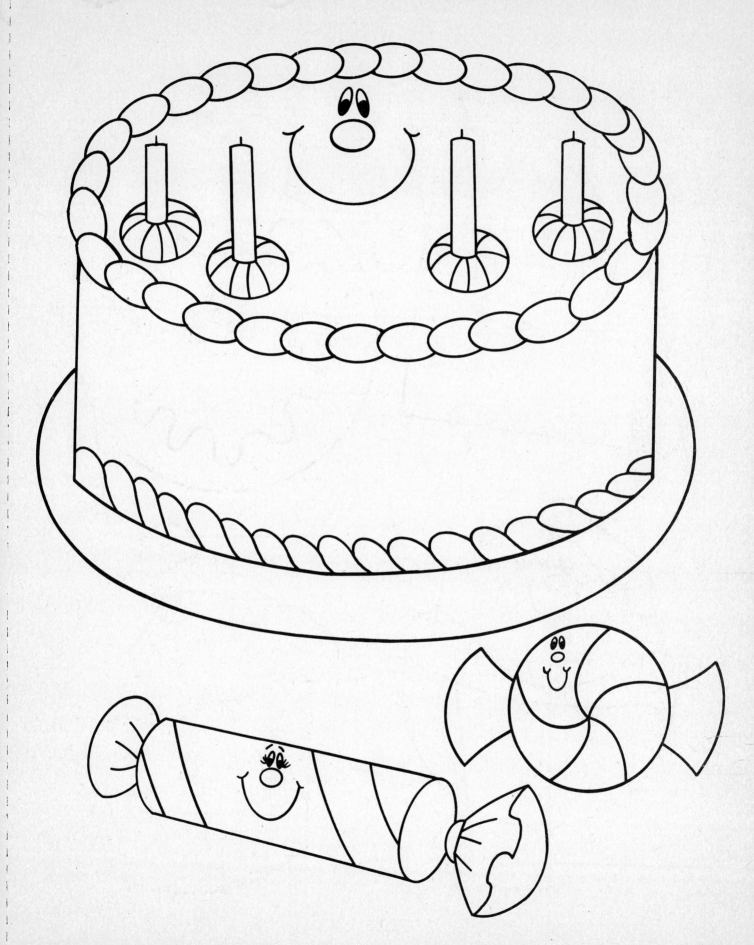

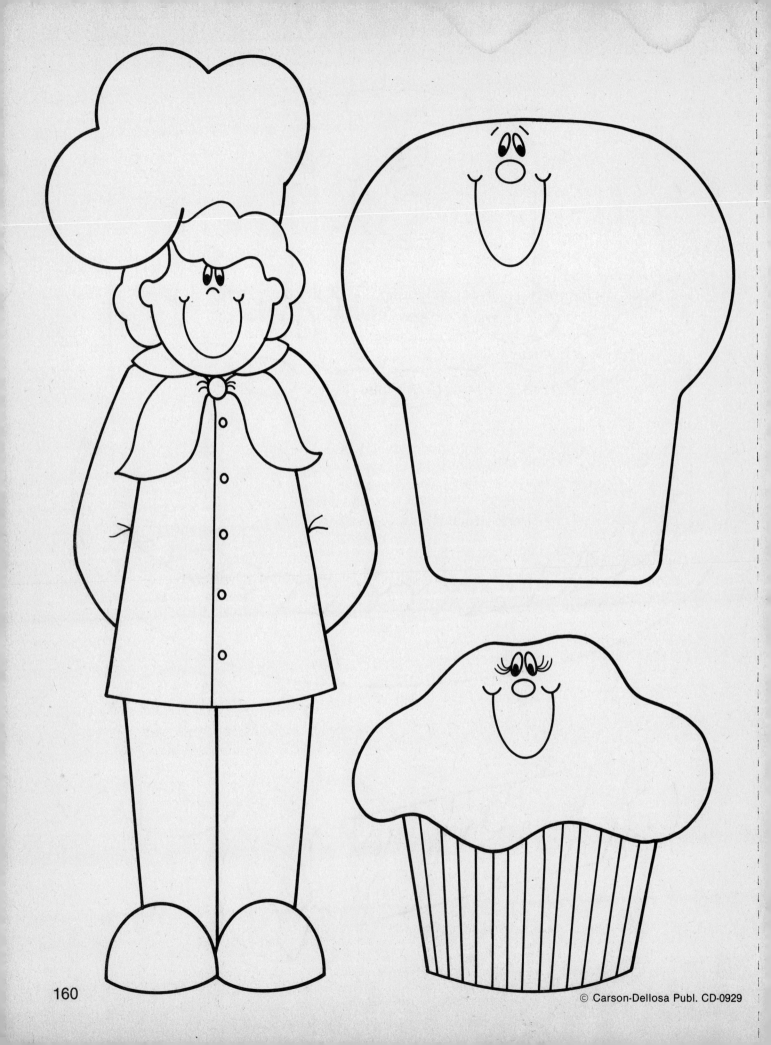

160